THE BIBLE IN THE LATIN WEST

THE MEDIEVAL BOOK

Volume One

THE BIBLE IN THE LATIN WEST

Margaret T. Gibson

UNIVERSITY OF NOTRE DAME
NOTRE DAME LONDON

Manufactured in the United States of America

Library of Congress Cataloging-in-Publication Data

Gibson, Margaret T.
The Bible in the Latin West / Margaret T. Gibson.
p. cm. — (The Medieval book ; v. 1)
Includes bibliographical references and index.
ISBN 0-268-00693-8 (alk. paper)
1. Bible. Latin—Versions—History. 2. Bible—Manuscripts, Latin. 3. Bible—Versions—History. I. Title. II. Series.
BS68.G534 1993
220.4'8'0902—dc20 92-56862
CIP

The paper used in this publication meets the minimum requirements of the American National Standard for Information Sciences—Permanence of Paper for Printed Library Materials, ANSI Z39.48-1984.

CONTENTS

PREFACE

The present volume is the first in a new series which addresses the codicology of texts; that is, how and why does the appearance of a manuscript change over the centuries? What questions should the student and scholar be prepared to ask to understand a manuscript in full? Where does the illumination fit in? *Habent sua fata libelli.* How much need we know of the later collections to which a manuscript has belonged, on the way to its final niche in the Bodleian Library?

As to the Latin Bible, the story told here begins in the great senatorial libraries of the later fourth century. None of these books has survived, but the principle of the sumptuous Pentateuch, Gospels or the complete Bible—no expense spared—derives from that senatorial tradition. I have kept to the 'straight' text of the Vulgate, with parallels in Greek and Hebrew, examples of vernacular versions, and some Latin commentary. Another book could be written on Latin and vernacular paraphrases in prose and verse from Late Antiquity onwards, and yet another on 'the Bible in pictures': the *Biblia pauperum* and the *Bible moralisée.* In the present volume illustration as such is less important than the colored and decorated initials that alert the reader to new books and new chapters in an age before the modern index.

I am indebted to the encouragement and guidance of many friends: among them François Avril, Bruce Barker-Benfield, Maureen Boulton, Michelle Brown, Carlotta Dionisotti, Peter Ganz, Anne Hudson, Kristian Jensen, Martin Kauffmann, Nigel Palmer, Clive Sneddon, Patricia Stirnemann. I am further indebted to the following libraries for permission to reproduce manuscripts and early printed books that are in their care: Bibliotheek der Rijksuniversiteit, Leiden; British Library, London; The National Trust, London; Bayerische Staatsbibliothek, Munich; University of Notre Dame, Notre Dame, Indiana; Bodleian Library, Oxford; Christ Church, Oxford; Bibliothèque Nationale, Paris; the William H. Scheide Library, Princeton, New Jersey; Stonyhurst College, Lancashire.

REFERENCES AND ABBREVIATIONS

In the descriptions accompanying the plates, abbreviated references are made to additional works fully cited in the bibliographies attached to each plate.

Bischoff, *Mittelalterliche Studien*	B. Bischoff, *Mittelalterliche Studien: ausgewählte Aufsätze zur Schriftkunde und Literaturgeschichte,* 3 vols. (Stuttgart, 1966–81).
BMC	*Catalogue of Books Printed in the XVth Century now in the British Museum,* 12 vols. (London, 1908–85).
Cahn	W. Cahn, *Romanesque Bible Illumination* (Cornell, 1982).
CCCM	Corpus Christianorum. Continuatio medievalis (Turnhout, 1971–).
CCSL	Corpus Christianorum. Series latina (Turnhout, 1954–).
CSEL	Corpus scriptorum ecclesiasticorum latinorum (Vienna, 1866–).
EEMF	Early English Manuscripts in Facsimile (Copenhagen, 1951–).
Emden, *BRUO*	A. B. Emden, *A Biographical Register of the University of Oxford to A.D. 1500,* 3 vols. (Oxford, 1957).
Emden, *1501–1540*	A. B. Emden, *A Biographical Register of the University of Oxford 1501–1540* (Oxford, 1974).
Fischer, *Lateinische Bibelhandschriften*	B. Fischer, *Lateinische Bibelhandschriften im frühen Mittelalter* (Vetus Latina, 11; Freiburg, 1985).
Fischer, 'Alkuin-Bibeln'	B. Fischer, 'Die Alkuin-Bibeln' in *Lateinische Bibelhandschriften,* pp. 203–403 (see also *Die Bibel von Moutier-Grandval, British Museum Add. MS 10546,* ed. J. Duft et al. [Bern, 1971], pp. 49–98).
Fischer, 'Amiatinus'	B. Fischer, 'Codex Amiatinus und Cassiodor' in *Lateinische Bibelhandschriften,* pp. 9–34; rpt. from *Biblische Zeitschrift* NS 6 (1962) 57–79.
Fischer, 'Bibelausgaben'	B. Fischer, 'Bibelausgaben des frühen Mittelalters' in *Lateinische Bibelhandschriften,* pp. 35–100, at 57–66 (rpt. from *La Bibbia nell'alto medioevo* [Settimane di studio del Centro italiano di studi sull'alto medioevo 10, 26 aprile–2 maggio 1962 (Spoleto, 1963)], pp. 519–600, at 545–57).
Fischer, 'Bibeltext'	B. Fischer, 'Bibeltext und Bibelreform unter Karl dem Grossen' in *Lateinische Bibelhandschriften,* pp. 102–202, rpt. from *Karl der Grosse: Lebenswerk*

	und Nachleben. Band II: Das geistige Leben, ed. B. Bischoff (Düsseldorf, 1965), pp. 156–216.
Goff	F. R. Goff, *Incunabula in American Libraries: A Third Census of Fifteenth-Century Books Recorded in North American Collections* (New York, rpt. 1973).
Hain	L. Hain, *Repertorium bibliographicum,* 4 vols. (Stuttgart, 1837; rpt. Milan, 1948). Supplement by W. A. Copinger, 3 vols. (London, 1895–1902; rpt. Milan, 1950). Additions by D. Reichling, 2 vols. (Palermo, 1904; rpt. Milan, 1953).
Light, 'Versions'	L. Light 'Versions et révisions du texte biblique', in *Le Moyen Age et la Bible,* ed. P. Riché and G. Lobrichon (Bible de tous les temps, 4; Paris 1984), pp. 55–93.
Lowe	E. A. Lowe, *Codices latini antiquiores,* 11 vols. and supplement (Oxford, 1934–71).
Mise en page	ed. H.-J. Martin and J. Vezin, *Mise en page et mise en texte du livre manuscrit* (Paris, 1990).
Monde latin antique	*Le monde latin antique et la Bible,* ed. J. Fontaine and C. Pietri (Bible de tous les temps, 2; Paris, 1984).
Munk Olsen	B. Munk Olsen and P. Petitmengin, 'Les bibliothèques et la transmission des textes', in Vernet below, pp. 414–35.
Pächt and Alexander	O. Pächt and J. J. G. Alexander, *Illuminated Manuscripts in the Bodleian Library Oxford,* 3 vols. (Oxford, 1966–73).
Petitmengin, *Amiatinus*	P. Petitmengin, 'Le *Codex Amiatinus*' in *Mise en page,* pp. 72–77.
Petitmengin, 'Les plus anciens manuscrits'	P. Petitmengin, 'Les plus anciens manuscrits de la Bible latine' in *Monde latin antique,* pp. 89–127.
Petitmengin, 'Saint Louis'	P. Petitmengin, 'La Bible de saint Louis' [= Paris, Bibliothèque Nationale, lat. 10426] in *Mise en page,* pp. 85–89.
PG	J.-P. Migne, *Patrologia graeca,* 161 vols. and supplement (Paris, 1857–1936).
PL	J.-P. Migne, *Patrologia latina,* 221 vols. and supplement (Paris, 1844–1974).
Proctor	R. G. C. Proctor, *An Index to the Early Printed Books in the British Museum: From the Invention of Printing to the Year MD. With Notes of Those in the Bodleian Library,* 2 vols. (London, 1898).
Quentin	ed. H. Quentin et al., *Biblia sacra iuxta latinam Vulgatam versionem* (Rome, 1926–) [latest volume 'Liber duodecim prophetarum', 1987].
Reynolds and Wilson	L. D. Reynolds and N. G. Wilson, *Scribes and Scholars: A Guide to the Transmission of Greek and Latin Literature,* 3rd ed. (Oxford, 1991).
SC	R. W. Hunt, F. Madan, H. H. E. Craster et al., *A Summary Catalogue of Western Manuscripts in the Bodleian Library at Oxford,* 7 vols. (Oxford, 1922–53).
Stegmüller, *Repertorium*	F. Stegmüller, *Repertorium Biblicum Medii Aevi,* 11 vols. (Madrid, 1950–80).
Verfasserlexikon	*Die deutsche Literatur des Mittelalters: Verfasserlexikon,* ed. C. Stöllinger-Löser (Berlin/New York, 1978–).

Vernet	A. Vernet, ed., *Histoire des bibliothèques françaises, 1: Les bibliothèques médiévales du VIe siècle à 1530* (Paris, 1989).
Watson, *British Library*	A. G. Watson, *Catalogue of Dated and Datable Manuscripts c. 700–1600 in the Department of Manuscripts, the British Library,* 2 vols. (London, 1979).
Watson, *Oxford*	A. G. Watson, *Catalogue of Dated and Datable Manuscripts c. 435–1600 in Oxford Libraries,* 2 vols. (Oxford, 1984).
Weber	R. Weber et al., ed., *Biblia sacra iuxta Vulgatam versionem,* 2nd ed., 2 vols. (Stuttgart, 1975).

INTRODUCTION

And he said unto me, Son of man, can these bones live?
And I answered, 'O Lord God, thou knowest.'
Again he said unto me, 'Prophesy upon these bones and say unto them:
O ye dry bones, hear the word of the Lord.' (Ezek. 37:3–4)

Ossa arida, audite verbum Domini.

Jerome translated Ezekiel at the turn of the fourth century: *c.* 390–405.[1] He had before him the Hebrew Bible, the Greek Septuagint (LXX) and the *Vetus latina* Old Testament.[2] On that basis he made a complete rendering of the Old Testament into Latin according to the Hebrew original—*ex hebraica veritate.* This is the Old Testament section of the Vulgate Bible. The New Testament existed primarily in the Greek 'original',[3] and here Jerome translated only the four Gospels: the rest of the Vulgate New Testament (Acts–Revelation) is an anonymous Latin version, no doubt by several hands. Here too there was a complex tradition, to enrich or corrupt the simple act of translation from Greek. Older Latin versions were further complicated by liturgical practice—e.g. the addition of 'Accipite et manducate' to Christ's words at the Last Supper.[4] Hebrew, Greek and Latin versions were not only linguistic channels of transmission; they expressed different cultures, each with its own interpretation of the word of God. To the Greek New Testament we should add the dependent Syriac versions, which are today a significant part of the Greek biblical inheritance of the Middle East after Jerome.

In his prefaces to various books of the Bible Jerome addresses the Christian intelligentsia on whose support he relied for the freedom to study: Damasus, in a sense the first 'establishment' pope,[5] Sophronius, Paula and her daughter Eustochium.[6] He was already providing for a public whose language of formal discourse was Latin: in the celebration of the liturgy, in education, in

---

[1] Quentin (1978) 15.209; J. N. D. Kelly, *Jerome: His Life, Writings and Controversies* (London, 1975), pp. 159–63.

[2] H. F. D. Sparks, 'Jerome as a Biblical Scholar' in *The Cambridge History of the Bible, I: From the Beginnings to Jerome,* ed. P. R. Ackroyd and C. F. Evans (Cambridge, 1970), pp. 510–41. The LXX is edited by A. Rahlfs, *Septuaginta: id est vetus testamentum graece iuxta LXX interpretes,* 2 vols. (Stuttgart, 1935); for a French translation and commentary on the LXX Pentateuch see M. Harl, *La Bible d'Alexandrie,* 5 vols. (Paris, 1989–). An edition of the *Vetus latina* by B. Fischer and the monks of Beuron is in progress (Freiburg, 1949–). For the legend of the LXX see L. F. Hartman, 'Septuagint' in *New Catholic Encyclopedia* 13.97.

[3] I.e., the first written *text* was in Greek, although the protagonists in the Gospels were speaking Aramaic and reading Hebrew.

[4] I Cor. 11:24: "Take, eat . . .": Weber 2.1781, citing manuscripts 'following Alcuin's exemplar' and the similar reading 'comedite' in the Léon Bible of *a.* 960.

[5] See H. Chadwick's sharp account of Damasus: *The Early Christian Church* (London, 1967), pp. 160–65.

[6] For a useful account of Jerome's prefaces see M. E. Schild, *Abendländische Bibelvorreden bis zur Lutherbibel* (Quellen und Forschungen zur Reformationsgeschichte, 39; Heidelberg, 1970), pp. 16–18.

public orations and in private literature, whether imaginative or philosophical.[7] But essentially Jerome worked for himself, because he was interested. He was more than a translator; he was a skilled and confident editor, who would not only determine the textually correct reading, but also (and here lies the rub) the reading that was the more interesting or the more edifying or stylistically the more felicitous. Jerome's principles as a translator emerge most clearly in his commentaries on the prophetic books of the Old Testament and on St. Matthew's Gospel. Here we can see how he understands his text and, fatally, what interests him to the point of affecting the Vulgate translation.[8] Here in Ezekiel's vision, he had the option of 'de his ossibus' or (with LXX) 'super haec ossa', which he preferred.[9] In countless small decisions of this kind—decisions of no theological import—Jerome not only shaped the Vulgate Bible, but established the canons of its textual criticism.

Jerome died in 420, as a monk in Bethlehem. Through the political chaos of the fifth century in the west his work endured, if only as rarely consulted manuscripts in secure Roman libraries. We know for instance that the papal library was a going concern under Agapetus (535–36),[10] and probably on through the sixth century. Only then, when every civil servant was formally Christian, does Jerome's Vulgate emerge as the norm. Other texts remain in use, particularly in north Africa:[11] but Jerome has the edge—an edge which the Islamic conquest of the southern and eastern Mediterranean in the seventh century will convert to outright supremacy.

A. LATE ANTIQUITY

Senatorial books

The age of Justinian (527–65) is a world of establishment Christianity: legal, administrative and—not least—in the visual arts. The degree to which the imperial court had taken over Christ and the Apostles, the angels, martyrs and saints may be seen in the ivory diptychs of the fifth and sixth centuries.[12] Here is Christ, not as the man who talked with his friends but as the eternal consul with the insignia of heaven, his angelic entourage being equally arrayed as court officials.[13] To be a bishop could now be a politically powerful and lucrative position. It is in this Justinianic world, which still encompassed (if precariously) both Greek east and Latin west, that western Bible manuscripts can first be observed as a coherent tradition. They are all by now books rather than rolls, and all written on parchment rather than papyrus.[14] They already are, or can be, luxury volumes.

---

[7]For the problems of 'Christian Latin' see succinctly Kelly, *Jerome,* p. 163.

[8]A notorious instance is Jerome's rendering of Exod. 34:29: 'Cumque descenderet Moses de monte Sinai tenebat duas tabulas testimonii, et ignorabat quod *cornuta* esset facies sua ex consortio sermonis dei.' The LXX has δεδόζασταί (was resplendent); but Jerome expands the Hebrew *qrn* not to *quāran* (shining) but to *quèrèn* (horned). His words were taken literally in representations of Moses from the eleventh century onwards (no. 10). See further R. Mellinkoff, *The Horned Moses in Medieval Art and Thought* (Berkeley, 1970).

[9]*S. Hieronymi presbyteri Commentariorum in Hiezechielem libri XIV,* ed. F. Glorie (CCSL, 75; Turnhout, 1964), p. 513.

[10]H.-I. Marrou, 'Autour de la bibliothèque du pape Agapit', *Mélanges d'archéologie et d'histoire* 48 Ecole Française de Rome (1931) 124–69, at 164–69.

[11]'Qui enim scripturas ex hebraea in graecam uerterunt, numerari possunt, latini autem interpretes nullo modo. Vt enim cuique primis fidei temporibus in manus uenit codex graecus et aliquantum facultatis sibi utriusque linguae habere uidebatur, ausus est interpretari' (*Sancti Aurelii Augustini. De doctrina christiana* (CCSL, 32; Turnhout, 1962) 2.16, p. 42; cf. 21–22).

[12]W. F. Volbach, *Elfenbeinarbeiten der Spätantike und des frühen Mittelalters,* 3rd ed. (Mainz, 1976), e.g. nos. 137 and 145; cf. 223–24.

[13]Volbach, *Elfenbeinarbeiten,* no. 109.

[14]Petitmengin, 'Les plus anciens manuscrits', 92. See further C. H. Roberts and T. C. Skeat, *The Birth of the Codex* (London, 1983).

Any manuscript is costly in materials and time, but the Tours Pentateuch (**no. 1**) has always been in the heirloom class: its milieu is the great senatorial house, with its festive plate, its chapel accoutrements and a library in which fine manuscripts, whether of the Bible or the Latin classics, served the same social and political need for display.

Cassiodorus

One such senator was Cassiodorus: historian, exegete, court official in Ravenna and one of the great creative librarians of the Latin west.[15] In his years of retirement (which ran to several decades: *c.* 530–80) Cassiodorus established in his ancestral villa near Naples a devout community, which he called Vivarium, after the water-gardens in its spacious grounds.[16] Like Benedict at Monte Cassino, Cassiodorus was responding to political instability, but in other respects the two monasteries were wholly dissimilar. Whereas Monte Cassino was a fortress, Vivarium had what might be described as 'all ancient conveniences': the supply of food and raw materials normal to a senatorial villa, a drainage system and a library. The rationale of the collection is set out in the *Institutiones:* sacred learning in Book I and secular learning in Book II. The Bible, Cassiodorus specified, is normally in nine volumes (*Inst.* I.11.3):

(i)	Genesis-Ruth
(ii)	the six books of Kings
(iii)	the four Major and twelve Minor Prophets
(iv)	the Psalter
(v)	Wisdom literature
(vi)	the lives of great men and women: Job, Tobit, Esther, Judith, Maccabees, Ezra-Nehemiah
(vii)	the four Gospels
(viii)	Pauline and Catholic Epistles
(ix)	Acts of the Apostles, the Apocalypse.

If it is deployed as a single massive volume in a large hand, that will be a book of 95 quires of eight (760 fol.);[17] in a smaller hand 53 quires of twelve (636 fol.) will suffice.[18] Every book has its commentary, in one or more separate volumes.[19] What Cassiodorus is describing is the traditional senatorial library as he had known it in Rome and Constantinople, and the established techniques of book-production as these had developed by the mid-sixth century. It was not a system that could survive the radical change and decay that the great senatorial families suffered in the barbarian west. Just as Vivarium had no ambitions to rival Monte Cassino in monastic asceticism, so its library was not intended to be either a model or a supply-center for the monastic libraries of western Europe. Vivarium flourished for thirty or forty years until Cassiodorus's death in 583; then, with the collapse of its economic support, the community vanished. So too did the library,

---

[15] A. Momigliano, 'Cassiodoro' in *Dizionario biografico degli Italiani* (1978) 21.494–504, with bibliography; and especially 'Cassiodorus and the Italian Culture of His Time', *Proceedings of the British Academy* 41 (1955) 207–245, rpt. in *Secondo contributo alla storia degli studi classici* (Rome, 1960), pp. 191–229. See also J. J. O'Donnell, *Cassiodorus* (Berkeley, 1979), reviewed by Averil Cameron in *Journal of Roman Studies* 71 (1981) 183–86; and now—involuted but indispensable—S. J. B. Barnish, 'The Work of Cassiodorus after His Conversion', *Latomus* 48 (1989) 157–87.

[16] *Cassiodori senatoris Institutiones*, ed. R. A. B. Mynors (Oxford, 1937) 1.29.1, p. 73.

[17] *Inst.* 1.14.2, p. 40 ('in codice grandiore littera clariore conscripto').

[18] *Inst.* 1.12.3, p. 37 ('minutiore manu').

[19] *Inst.* 1.11.3, p. 36 ('paene cum omnibus latinis expositoribus suis'). See further *Inst.* 1.1–9, pp. 11–34.

as a coherent collection of books; but the *Institutiones* survived as a fund of information, and a marker for patrons and librarians of the future.[20]

Bede

A pandect of the Bible, a 95-quire *codex grandior,* reached northern England *c.* 680, where it generated three direct copies. One of these survives intact as the Codex Amiatinus, another is the eleven leaves of the 'Ceolfrid Bible' in the British Library, arguably the third survives as 'the Bankes leaf', now in the possession of the National Trust (**no. 3**).[21] Although Bede seems to have been unaware of the *Institutiones* as a text,[22] he could examine a *codex grandior* in the original and observe its recreation, down to the details of ruling, spacing and paragraphing, by the scribes of Monkwearmouth and Jarrow. Other manuscripts from late antique Italy and the Mediterranean that were brought to Northumbria in Bede's lifetime included material in Greek. The manuscript of Acts (**no. 2**), which Bede almost certainly used to revise his own commentary, gave him and his readers the sense of immediate contact with the Greek original. Indeed if the study of Greek in Canterbury under Theodore and Hadrian amounted to anything—and there is emerging evidence that it did[23]—we can scarcely credit that in the north Bede remained isolated and ignorant. If only in Nothelm, he had a channel to the materials and methods of the school of Theodore.[24] So the exegetical traditions of Late Antiquity persisted in a land which Cassiodorus might well have termed 'ultima Thule'.

Cuthbert

Lindisfarne is more remote still. By Bede's lifetime it had lost its political eminence in the English church, and only by the happy accident of the life and cult of St. Cuthbert did it remain on the ecclesiastical map. The Lindisfarne Gospels (**no. 4**) were written and illuminated in the service

[20] M. Cappuyns, 'Cassiodore' in *Dictionnaire d'histoire et géographie ecclésiastique* 11.1388–92, 1398–99. No original manuscript from Cassiodorus's library is now thought to be extant.

[21] That the Bankes leaf is the sole witness to Ceolfrid's third pandect is still a matter of scholarly dispute. On the one hand, it came to light in Dorset as a binding fragment to sixteenth-century estate records of the Willoughby family, among whose Nottinghamshire records were preserved the eleven leaves of London, British Library, MS Add. 45025; *ergo* 'Bankes' is part of the same manuscript. The other fragment, British Library MS Add. 37777, was bought by Canon Greenwell in Newcastle. Thus the antiquarian context is: Willoughby in Dorset ('Bankes'), Willoughby in Nottinghamshire (MS Add. 45025) and Greenwell in Newcastle (MS Add. 37777). Against this antiquarian coincidence of Willoughby estate records may, and should, be set the evidence of script and *mise-en-page.* The Bankes leaf differs from the other British Library fragments in having no vertical ruling, in being by a different scribe (although he is observing the same conventions), and in its later medieval chapter-divisions; these are by another hand, who rarely or never favored highlighting the opening line. These are real obstacles, which could be set aside only by the discovery in *Amiatinus* of features that distinguish the Bankes leaf. For details compare MS Add. 37777: recto reproduced by Petitmengin, *Amiatinus,* p. 34, verso reproduced by E. A. Lowe, *English Uncial* (Oxford, 1960), no. 10. Note for instance: **L** and **F** (MS Add. 37777, forked tail); **B** ('Bankes', bow not completed); **G** (contrasting treatment of tail). Most convenient of all, contrast the abbreviating line over *ds* and *dns.* Of the two scribes 'Bankes' is the more skilled and confident.

[22] The *Institutiones* are not listed by M. L. W. Laistner, 'The Library of the Venerable Bede' in *Bede: His Life, Times and Writings,* ed. A. Hamilton Thompson (Oxford, 1935), pp. 237–66.

[23] Bede himself testifies to the proficiency of the pupils of Theodore and Hadrian in both Latin and Greek: '. . . usque hodie supersunt de eorum discipulis, qui Latinam Graecamque linguam aeque ut propriam in qua nati sunt norunt': *Historia ecclesiastica,* ed. B. Colgrave and R. A. B. Mynors (Oxford, 1969), 4.2, p. 334. For Bede's own access to Greek see A. C. Dionisotti, 'On Bede, Grammars, and Greek', *Revue bénédictine* 92 (1982) 111–41; and for the field as a whole see B. Bischoff and M. Lapidge, *The Milan Glosses* (CCCM, forthcoming).

[24] See Bede, *In regum librum XXX quaestiones,* ed. D. Hurst, (CCSL, 119; Turnhout, 1962).

of that cult. The script is deliberately insular rather than Roman (contrast **no. 3**); the full-page miniatures of the Evangelists show how the late antique author-portrait could be adapted to the two-dimensional art of the north. Here the Mediterranean exemplar has been acclimatized rather than replicated. Yet Cuthbert himself owned a pocket gospelbook in purest uncial (**no. 4**).[25] The community at Lindisfarne *c.* 700 lived in two worlds: the still potent vestiges of the Roman Empire and the Germanic and Celtic North.

B. THE CAROLINGIANS

Fulda

The great English foundation in continental Europe was Fulda: not in its original establishment by the disciples of Boniface in 744, but as the political beneficiary of Charlemagne's Saxon wars, and thus the center of patronage for the whole area of what is now Hesse and Lower Saxony. Like seventh-century England, this was a mission-field, in which Boniface and his successors established literacy and taught the faith. For books they turned to England and Rome, primarily indeed to England. Although there was papal support for the German mission, it was essentially an English endeavor: the liturgy and practice, the books and script are thus Roman at one remove. Greek texts are inaccessible. It is the more interesting that one of the first scholarly texts to reach Fulda was the Latin version of Tatian's *Diatessaron,* which was made in 545/6 for Victor, bishop of Capua. The manuscript appears to be Victor's original, salvaged by some Anglo-Saxon bibliophile and still extant as testimony to Fulda's role in preserving and transmitting the biblical scholarship of Antiquity.[26]

Canon Tables

A harmony (like Tatian's) altered and abridged the sacred text. In principle the Gospels could be correlated without such alteration by the construction of preliminary canon-tables (**no. 5**), reinforced by marginalia at the corresponding points in the text. Canon-tables were also an opportunity for quite elaborate figural embellishment, such as Evangelist-portraits or initials with zoomorphic interlace. This opening fanfare complements a text in which the sole means of decoration is a hierarchy of scripts and the alternation of gold and red inks.

Theodulf of Orleans

In the late eighth century Rome was fleetingly rebuilt north of the Alps. The palace at Aachen became Charlemagne's principal residence, a legal, fiscal and archival center, and visually an expression of his royal and imperial power. Aachen was the center of government and, within that greater whole, the center of both learning *per se* and the provision and exchange of books.[27] One

---

[25]The pocket gospelbook in itself is an insular, indeed Irish, phenomenon, as is its cultic association with a local saint.

[26]*CLA,* no. 1196. 'Glossator A' in this Fulda manuscript has been identified with St. Boniface himself: M. B. Parkes, 'The Handwriting of St. Boniface: A Reassessment of the Problems', *Beiträge zur Geschichte der deutsche Sprache und Literatur* 98 (Tübingen 1976) 161–79; reprinted in *Scribes, Scripts and Readers: Studies in the Communication, Presentation and Dissemination of Medieval Texts* (London, 1991), pp. 121–42.

[27]See in general B. Bischoff, *Karl der Grosse: Lebenswerk und Nachleben. Band II: Das geistige Leben* (Düsseldorf, 1964); for Charlemagne's library, see Bischoff, 'Die Hofbibliothek Karls des Grossen' (rpt. in Bischoff, *Mittelalterliche Studien* 3.149–69). A list of classical texts from the court library survives in Berlin, Staatsbibliothek Preussischer Kulturbesitz, MS

scholar who sought Charlemagne's patronage in these years was Theodulf, a Visigoth from Islamic Spain. In that he became bishop of Orleans and an imperial envoy to Rome, Theodulf is likely to have come of a solid aristocratic family, its fortunes no doubt diminished by two generations of Islamic rule. He was an imaginative patron, a good occasional poet,[28] and—more surprisingly—an editor of the Latin Bible. His revision of the Vulgate (**no. 6**) illustrates very well the strengths and the limitations of textual criticism in his day. He had good Latin, a gut instinct for detecting error and an interest in variant readings; but without Hebrew and Greek he had no linguistic security, nor had he any theory of emendation that we can discern. Even so, Theodulf's belief in the propriety of verifying and emending the text of Scripture is comparable with the zeal of his younger contemporary, Lupus of Ferrières, as an editor of Cicero[29]—and may indeed be considered more remarkable.

Alcuin

'Alcuin Bibles' (**no. 7**) are something of a misnomer, in that the genre did not stabilize until fifteen or twenty years after Alcuin's death (804). Some thirty in all are still extant, written in St. Martin's, Tours, in the abbacies of Alcuin himself, Fridugisus (807–34), Adalhard and Vivian (*ob.* 851).[30] To look at, they are massive folio lectern Bibles in one or two volumes. Some are lavishly illustrated, others plain: but so far as we know (and we know too little) they have a common text. Most of them were exported to other houses in northern France and the Rhineland, where they might serve as exemplars for further pandects in the Tours style.[31] Thus while the text of the 'Alcuin Bibles' is in no sense official (e.g. as known at the court of Charlemagne or Louis the Pious) or definitive, it is both stable and widely diffused. In practice—and by default—it represents the standard text of the Carolingian Bible, outside Italy.

Rabanus Maurus

Alcuin's star pupil was Rabanus Maurus, 'the black raven' from Saxony.[32] Rabanus was sent to Aachen to study with Alcuin and, it may be thought, to confirm his political fidelity to those who mattered. He is a rare instance of the scholar-statesman who was truly successful in both aspects of his life. As abbot of Fulda he had the charge, direct or indirect, of six hundred monks; as archbishop of Mainz his province stretched along the Main, up to the Elbe and infinitely beyond. To the west, he had to fight his corner with the archbishop of Rheims, Ebbo and then the more dangerous Hincmar. It is a measure of Rabanus's mental stamina as well as his range and originality that he not only wrote practical letters and treatises in the line of his ecclesiastical duty, he also constructed an encyclopedia of universal knowledge and commented on nearly the entire Bible. His biblical commentary (**no. 8**) was not new, but neither was it mindless plagiarism. The revision and clarification of the Fathers, so that they might be intelligible to modern readers, was initiated by Bede, continued by Alcuin and to a remarkable degree stabilized by Rabanus. So Cassiodorus's

---

Diez. B. Sant. 66, pp. 218–19 (see the facsimile of the manuscript in B. Bischoff, *Grammatici latini et catalogus librorum* [Codices selecti, 42; Graz, 1973]).

[28]See P. Godman, *Poetry of the Carolingian Renaissance* (London, 1985), 'Introduction' and pp. 150–74, with references.

[29]Facsimile ed. C. H. Beeson, *Lupus of Ferrières as Scribe and Text Critic: A Study of His Autograph Copy of Cicero's De oratore* (Cambridge, Mass., 1930).

[30]Fischer, 'Alkuin-Bibeln', pp. 256–59.

[31]See note 35 below.

[32]W. Selzer, 'Der Name Rabanus' in *Rabanus Maurus in seiner Zeit, 780–1980* (Catalogue of an Exhibition, 13 September–19 October 1980; Mainz, 1980), pp. 61–62.

advice remained valid: that a good library should contain a careful text of the Bible, with a commentary to each book.

C. THE VERNACULAR

The three learned languages — the languages in which Christ's title had been written on the Cross — were Latin, Greek and Hebrew. Already in the fourth century there were Bible translations into eastern vernaculars, notably Syriac, and into Gothic, the language of the barbarian overlords of Italy and Spain. The Goths were Arians, and perhaps for this reason the Gothic Bible scarcely survived the sixth century. But the need remained: to render the Bible intelligible not only to the Romance-speakers of Italy, Gaul and Spain, who could all make a good shot at the Latin, but to the Germanic north, which had no point of linguistic contact. Franks and Burgundians, Anglo-Saxons and Lombards all had to learn Latin as a new written language. Not everyone could do so; and we assume that from the beginning of the conversions there was extensive translation. Initially the most effective medium was verse. Barbarian societies had an oral tradition of heroic poetry — whether history, elegy or panegyric — into which the vernacular Bible could readily be adopted and acclimatized, without (in all probability) being written down. So the unlettered Caedmon was miraculously endowed with the gift of epic narrative:

> The angel said, 'Cedmon, sing me hwaethwigu.'
> Tha ondswaerede he & cwaeth, 'Ne con ic noht singan; & ic forthon of theossum gebeorscipe uteode, & hider gewat, forthon ic naht singan ne cuthe.'
> Eft he cwaeth se the with hine sprecende waes, 'Hwaethre thu meaht singan.'
> Tha cweath he, 'Hwaet sceal ic singan?'
> Cwaeth he, 'Sing me frumsceaft.'
> Tha he thas andsware onfeng, tha ongon he sona singan in herenesse Godes Scyppendes tha fers & tha word the he naefre gehyrde. . . .
> *Na sculon herigan heofonrices weard,*
> *meotodes meahte & his modgethanc*
> *weorc wuldorfaeder. . . .*[33]

Declamation of the Scriptures in verse persisted through the eighth century, in parallel with *Beowulf.* Whenever that died out (and the date is quite uncertain) it was replaced only with the Psalter (**no. 11**) and some passages from the Pentateuch and the Gospels. Translation of the Bible as such was addressed systematically only by Aelfric and his colleagues *c.* 1000 (**no. 10**), and even they achieved nothing like the complete Bible.

Scholia

What does survive from the early period is interlinear scholia: in Anglo-Saxon, in Old Irish and in Old High German. These are normally one-to-one above the relevant Latin word, providing translations, variant interpretations, marks of emphasis, cross-references: all the paraphernalia of close textual study in a foreign language. Complete interlinear translations of some books of the Bible are found from the ninth century onwards. The Vespasian Psalter acquired an English gloss,

---

[33] T. Miller, *The Old English Version of Bede's 'Ecclesiastical History of the English People'* (Early English Text Society, 95; London, 1890), Part 1, pp. 342–44; cf. Bede, *Historia ecclesiastica,* ed. B. Colgrave and R. A. B. Mynors (Oxford, 1969) 4.24, pp. 414–19.

as eventually did the Lindisfarne Gospels (**no. 4**). The more elegant option was to plan a two-language manuscript from the start, either in two columns or on facing pages. Although the precedent had long been available in Graeco-Latin manuscripts of the Psalter, the Pauline Epistles and the Acts of the Apostles (**no. 2**), only one manuscript is known with Latin and Anglo-Saxon in parallel, the beautiful and unusual 'Paris Psalter' of the mid-eleventh century (**no. 11**).

Christian epic

In 1531 Beatus Rhenanus went to Freising in search of manuscripts of Livy, apparently without success. But he used his time in the still-intact monastic library and lit upon a manuscript of Otfrid's *Evangelienbuch* (**no. 9**).

> All credit [he wrote trenchantly] to the *Franci* of long ago, who undertook the translation of the Bible into their own language, namely German; there are theologians of our own time who cannot accept so much.[34]

Otfrid's *Evangelienbuch,* written in Weissenburg in northern Alsace about 860, survives in a fine contemporary copy now in Vienna, and in several of the next generation. It was written for a courtly audience, such as the archbishop of Mainz and King Louis 'the German' in Regensburg. Such men and women had a working knowledge of Latin, both spoken and written; but they enjoyed the perspective of the epic narrative. The fact of the *Evangelienbuch*'s being in German was far less important than its heroic style. Conversely Otfrid's sound Latin scholarship, to which there is ample testimony, underpinned the language and the doctrine of the *Evangelienbuch.* Two hundred years later this tradition of scholarly amity between Latin and German is still vigorous in the translation and commentary of Williram of Ebersberg (**no. 12**).

D. MONASTIC BIBLES

Whereas in early medieval Europe (north of the Alps) the monasteries were as central to learning and literacy as they were to political and economic life, by the twelfth century monastic life and scholarship was imperceptibly becoming detached from the wider world. Although that separation was never absolute, it distinguishes the classic book-production of the eleventh and twelfth centuries, which is that of the monastic *scriptoria,* from newer developments among the secular clergy, in schools and universities and in the lay world beyond. The monastic Bible may be a complete pandect for public use, or a series of individual books or groups of books for private study. *Plus ça change, plus c'est la même chose.* The distinction is in principle to be found in Cassiodorus's *Institutiones,* a text that was certainly available to eleventh- and twelfth-century scholars, though they do not quote it much.

Display Bibles

Although pandects had never gone entirely out of fashion,[35] the great era for their production was *c.* 1060–1160. Stately two-column folios that hark back to *Amiatinus* in their dimensions (about

---

[34]'Perpetua vero laus Francorum veterum qui sacros libros in suam, hoc est Germanicam linguam vertendos curarint, quod nuper a Theologis quibusdam improbatum scimus' (Beatus Rhenanus, *Rerum germanicarum libri tres* [Basel, 1531], p. 108).

[35]Carl Nordenfalk identified Hildesheim, Domschatz MS 61 as having a Tours Bible as its exemplar: 'Noch ein tu-

450 x 300 mm.), they were normally in two volumes, splendidly bound (**no. 13**). They are bigger than Carolingian Bibles, their internal decoration is more extensive,[36] and their script is much more even. Whether their text is any better is another question. Every self-respecting monastery had one, either made locally or imported from the relatively few *scriptoria* that had the resources, the scribes and the illuminators to maintain the stability of script and initials over five hundred pages. The social context of these great pandects is still to be explored. A bishop of the Gregorian reform (it has been suggested)[37] might appropriately have given such a volume to a community that he had restored: statutes rewritten, estates reorganized, personnel replaced—plus a first-class Bible. But this Gregorian argument can only partly explain why the fashion throughout Europe swung towards the display Bible. Gospelbooks were out, Bibles in; not everywhere simultaneously, but nearly everywhere in the end.[38]

The 'Glossa ordinaria'

The *Glossed Bible* (**no. 14**) is the latest and most successful invention of the monastic *scriptorium,* achieving its classic form *c.* 1140–*c.* 1160. It consists of nine or ten volumes containing individual books of the Bible, or several related books (e.g. all or part of the Pentateuch, the Wisdom-literature, the Gospels), each having marginal and interlinear annotation throughout. In substance the annotation derives from the Latin Fathers; the *Gloss* is a summary of patristic exegesis, visually deployed so that the relevant gloss is always closely adjacent to its text.[39] The elegant presentation and stable text reflect wealthy and experienced *scriptoria,* such as in northern Europe must be monastic.[40] But the market was wider: bishops and the higher clergy, aristocratic collectors and (crucially) the masters expounding the Bible in the emergent universities. For the last time, the traditional Benedictine monastery had a key role to play in book-production.[41]

Nicholas of Lyra

While the *Glossed Bible* was indispensable, it offered, so to say, the classic analysis of Scripture: its method and outlook that of Late Antiquity—philosophically neoplatonist, and often more interested in the allegorical value of a text than in its literal meaning. The professional study of the Bible in Paris and Oxford and in the new universities of the thirteenth and fourteenth centuries made two demands that the *Glossed Bible* could not satisfy: the integration of all data within a theological system, and the clarification of the literal meaning. The former led to the *Summa theologiae* of Aquinas and away from the Bible text as such. The latter need was met by Hugh of St. Cher O.P. and Alexander of Hales O.F.M. and their successors, but definitively by a Franciscan scholar of the next generation, Nicholas of Lyra. The *Postillae litterales* (**no. 15**), which he gave as lectures

---

ronische Bilderbibel' in *Festschrift Bernhard Bischoff zu seinem 65. Geburtstag,* ed. J. Autenrieth and F. Brunhölzl (Stuttgart, 1971), pp. 153–63; M. Stähli and H. Härtel, *Die Handschriften im Domschatz zu Hildesheim* (Wiesbaden, 1984), pp. 147–66.

[36]I mean initials within the text rather than full-page illumination.

[37]Cahn, pp. 102–104.

[38]Fine examples are the great Winchester Bible (*c.* 1150–1180) and the related Auct. Bible (C. M. Kauffmann, *Romanesque Manuscripts, 1066–1190* [A Survey of Manuscripts Illuminated in the British Isles, 3; London, 1975], nos. 83 and 82; W. Oakeshott, *The Two Winchester Bibles* [Oxford, 1981]; Pächt and Alexander 3.128). The value of such Bibles is well captured by the story of Henry II's 'gift' of the Winchester Bible to Witham Priory in Somerset (Oakeshott, pp. 33–34).

[39]M. T. Gibson and K. Froehlich, *Biblia latina cum Glossa ordinaria* (Louvain, 1992) [facsimile of the *editio princeps* of the *Glossed Bible,* 1480].

[40]The *Glossed Bible* south of the Alps is still a closed book.

[41]The role of monastic houses in providing exemplars and establishing editions for the early printers (e.g. **no. 16**) has still to be explored.

in Paris in the 1320s and then published,[42] served as the basic source of practical information on Scripture for the next two hundred years. They were printed eight years before the *Glossed Bible* itself,[43] and then triumphantly combined with the *Gloss* on the same page (**no. 16**) with the Fathers above, Lyra below.

Nicholas was a modern scholar working in the University of Paris; he was also, and primarily, a member of a religious order which supplied his books and commanded his time. Indispensable though such men were to the medieval university, both in teaching and research, they were peripheral to its formal constitution. It was the secular masters who 'were' the university,[44] and who were responsible for its internal jurisdiction, its finances and its curriculum.

E. THE UNIVERSITY TEXT

Peter Lombard

Peter Lombard was bishop of Paris for a bare year in 1159; he died at the juncture of his career between teaching in the school of Notre Dame and participating in the juridical establishment of the University of Paris.[45] He had long been more than plain 'scholasticus' in the cathedral chapter. He was the major exponent of the Bible in the Paris of the 1150s, lecturing on the Psalter and the Pauline Epistles (**no. 17**), and across the spectrum of theology, ethics and canon law. In this latter field his *Sententiarum libri IV* were adopted as the definitive collection, on which every regent master in theology was required to give a course of lectures. It is the textbook *par excellence* for theology students from the late twelfth century to the mid-fourteenth and beyond.[46] By contrast, his expositions of the Psalter and the Pauline Epistles, though widely available into the fourteenth century and beyond, were not formally adopted as texts for study; they were books for scholarly consultation, like the *Glossed Bible* itself.

Lecturing on the Bible

To what extent did anyone lecture on the Bible? The Psalter and the Pauline Epistles were undoubtedly the subject of formal exposition in Paris *c.* 1140–*c.* 1160; the commentaries of Gilbert de la Porrée and Peter Lombard are sufficient testimony. Whether this tradition was incorporated in later university practice is another question. At first sight, yes. Stephen Langton lectured repeatedly and comprehensively on the Bible *c.* 1180–*c.* 1200 (**no. 18**).[47] He analyzed the literal meaning of a passage of Scripture, and its reflection *moraliter* in the individual soul and *allegoriter* in the Church. His cross-references from one chapter of the Bible to another helped to establish the

[42] Several notes and colophons throughout the work indicate progress: at Gen. 1.27, 1322; at III Esdras, 13 kal. April 1330; at Ezekiel, 1332. See in detail H. Labrosse, 'Sources de la biographie de Nicolas de Lyre', *Études franciscaines* 16 (1906) at pp. 386–87 and 'Oeuvres de Nicolas de Lyre', *Études franciscaines* 19 (1908) at pp. 157–58.

[43] Sweynheym and Pannartz, Rome 1472, quickly followed by Mentelin, Strassburg 1473. Details in *BMC* 1.56 (Mentelin) and 4.14 (Sweynheym, Pannartz) respectively.

[44] The notable exception is Bologna, where the students constituted the university: see H. Rashdall, *The Universities of Europe in the Middle Ages,* ed. F. M. Powicke and A. B. Emden, 3 vols. (Oxford, 1936) 1.148–51; with further bibliography in section E below.

[45] M. Colish, *Peter Lombard* (forthcoming); with further bibliography in section E below.

[46] *Sententiae in IV libris distinctae,* ed. Pp. Collegii S. Bonaventurae ad Claras Aquas, 2 vols. (Spicilegium bonaventurianum 4–5; Grottaferrata, 1971–81). For its use see F. Stegmüller, *Repertorium commentariorum in Sententias Petri Lombardi,* 2 vols. (Würzburg, 1947), 1.x-xi.

[47] B. Smalley, *The Study of the Bible in the Middle Ages,* 3rd ed. (Oxford, 1983), chap. 5.

chapter-divisions with which we are familiar today.[48] Such material was appropriate to students who might have a regular preaching commitment as secular clergy. But it may be doubted whether any but the most diligent and well-funded followed the entire series from Genesis to the Apocalypse. For men in a hurry the *seriatim* commentary was far less useful than the collection of *distinctiones,* used in conjunction with the Bible itself and a good concordance.[49]

The Friars

It has been shrewdly observed that in the early thirteenth century the only security for a man who wished to pursue research (biblical or otherwise) was to become a friar. Thereby he was guaranteed subsistence and modern library facilities for life.[50] So the great Dominican research center was established in the rue Saint Jacques: there Hugh of St. Cher revised and further developed Langton's commentaries, and Thomas Aquinas found the materials for his exposition of the Gospels.[51] There too Vincent of Beauvais organized the *équipe* that began to assemble, systematize and transcribe his encyclopedic *Speculum* of knowledge.[52] Men of equal distinction were to be found at the Franciscan house of study in the rue des Cordeliers: Alexander of Hales, John of La Rochelle, Bonaventure and subsequently Nicholas of Lyra.[53] It was a practical decision by William of Auvergne in 1230 as bishop of Paris to allow these scholarly friars, who were not strictly members of the university, to hold teaching positions in the Faculty of Theology.[54]

Paris Bibles

In this era of expansion and discovery the most characteristic product of the Paris book trade was the so-called 'Paris Bible'.[55] By the thirteenth century the monastic *scriptorium* had been replaced by the secular workshop in which books were written and illuminated both to the order of a patron and for the open market.[56] It supplied both the texts specific to the university and the basic works of reference for a scholar's private library. The speculative risks were small: a dozen manuscripts rather than a print-run of five hundred. But however modest the scale, this is the milieu in which 'Paris Bibles' were first developed, and continued to be produced throughout the thirteenth and early fourteenth centuries. They came to be made throughout northern France and even in En-

---

[48]The dictum that Stephen Langton divided the Bible into chapters cannot be directly substantiated, e.g. by contemporary observations, colophons, autograph notes. Langton's chapter-divisions can be clearly seen within his commentaries; the same divisions are normal within the 'Paris Bibles' (see below); and they are imposed by thirteenth- and fourteenth-century readers on older manuscripts. Their universal adoption owes more to the standard practice of 'Paris Bibles' than to Langton himself.

[49]R. H. and M. A. Rouse, '*Statim invenire:* Schools, Preachers and New Attitudes to the Page' in *Renaissance and Renewal in the Twelfth Century,* ed. R. L. Benson and G. Constable with C. D. Lanham (Cambridge, Mass., 1982), pp. 201–223.

[50] R. W. Southern, *Western Society and the Church in the Middle Ages* (London, 1970), p. 294. A traditional Benedictine monastery would have required a sizeable entry fee, and had no regular access to books outside its own library. Cistercian houses were briefly attractive to academics in the later twelfth century, and some Augustinian houses met the same need; but from about 1220 the friars had it.

[51]For Hugh see his works; for Aquinas see J. Weisheipl, *Friar Thomas d'Aquino: His Life, Thought and Works* (Oxford, 1974), chap. 3 *et passim.*

[52]See conveniently J. Weisheipl, 'Vincent of Beauvais' in *New Catholic Encyclopedia* (1967) 14.679–80. It is not yet clear how much of the work was done in Paris and how much at Royaumont, O.Cist., near Beauvais.

[53]J. G. Bougerol, *Introduction à l'étude de saint Bonaventure* (Tournai, 1961), pp. 48–50, with references.

[54]N. Valois, *Guillaume d'Auvergne* (Paris, 1880), chap. 5.

[55]Light, 'Versions'.

[56]For the *status questionis* of the treacherous subject of books provided for and approved by the University of Paris see R. Marichal, 'Les manuscrits universitaires' in *Mise en page,* pp. 210–17.

gland, but the specification remains Parisian. These little books are multifarious in their text and illustrations, diverse in provenance and ownership. What they have in common is a thin, flexible parchment (which is almost certainly a single skin split in two) and a small, though not minute, script. Thus the entire Bible is contained in an octavo volume on (in modern terms) 'India paper'. That Parisian workshops had a leading part in developing the technology of 'Paris Bibles' need not be doubted. They established an accepted order and division of books,[57] some degree of uniformity in the text,[58] and the scale of the illumination, though not its iconography. Other centers of production borrowed and contributed; scribes and illuminators moved from place to place, no doubt with pattern-books. A good analogy is 'Limoges enamel', a term conveniently applicable to a far wider and more complex range of metal work than can reasonably be deemed to have been made within the city of Limoges. These are the first Bibles to be easily available across a wide social spectrum: to the wealthy bourgeoisie as much as to professional clerics and religious. They were to be superseded only by the yet more successful Book of Hours (**no. 22**).

Hebraica veritas

A genre in complete contrast to the ever more accessible Vulgate Bible is the bilingual Hebrew-Latin manuscript of the Old Testament (**no. 20**). These manuscripts were written by Latin scribes who had to some degree mastered Hebrew; they remained a specialized interest shared by a few university masters, a few monks, and (briefly) by an entire college of missionary friars.[59] They were a useful tool in the study of Hebrew as late as the 1520s.[60]

F. THE NEW LITERACY

The Bible in French

The language of day-to-day communication in thirteenth-century Paris—academic as well as practical—was French. It was in French that sermons were delivered, though normally they were recorded in Latin; and it was in French that the audiences of these sermons (at whatever level) habitually thought. So it is not surprising that virtually *pari passu* with the 'Paris Bible' (**no. 19**) in Latin the entire Bible was translated into French.[61] Again, no names are attached to the work: we can say only that the milieu is the Parisian intelligentsia *c.* 1235–60.[62] Textually almost everything remains to be clarified: the Latin base, the recourse to traditional commentary (e.g. from the *Glossa ordinaria*), the influence on later translations. Nor were vernacular Bibles as such universally ac-

---

[57] Petitmengin, 'Saint Louis'.

[58] Light, 'Versions'.

[59] Clement V (in 1311 at the Council of Vienne) and John XXII encouraged the establishment of chairs in Hebrew, Arabic and Aramaic at the curia itself, and in the universities of Paris, Oxford, Bologna and Salamanca (*Sexti Decretales* 5.1.1; Denifle, *Chartularium* 2.1.293). The missionary college flourished briefly in Majorca from 1274 to about 1290 (see John XXII's bull of 1276 to James II, king of Majorca). For a survey with further references see R. Sugranyes de Franch, *Raymond Lulle, docteur des missions* (Schöneck-Beckenried, 1954), pp. 65ff.

[60] An important group of Hebrew-Latin manuscripts has long been in Corpus Christi College, Oxford (manuscripts 5–11), the gift of John Claymond, the first Principal (Emden, *BRUO*, pp. 428–30). Claymond acquired them perhaps with the intention of teaching himself Hebrew.

[61] Other developments, which cannot be discussed here and which are quite distinct from the translation of the full Bible text, are: (a) the *Bible moralisée*, early thirteenth century, Parisian and primarily pictures; see now conveniently H. W. Stork, *Bible Moralisée: Codex Vindobonensis 2554 der Österreichischen Nationalbibliothek, Transkription und Übersetzung* (Saarbrücker Hochschulschriften, 9, Kunstgeschichte; Cologne/St. Ingbert, 1988); (b) the *Biblia pauperum*, mid-thirteenth-century South German, again primarily pictorial; see A. Henry, *Biblia pauperum* (London, 1987), with references.

ceptable.[63] But there can be no doubt that this early French Bible supplied the base text for the *Bible historiale complétée* (**no. 21**), that fusion of scriptural text and 'modern'[64] commentary without which no late medieval royal or aristocratic library was complete.

The Bible in English

The library of Geoffrey Chaucer (*ob.* 1400) consisted of works in Latin and French, with a bare handful of books in English. His own romances and the cycle of *Canterbury Tales* were written for a clientele in London who wanted their entertainment in English, but who could certainly also read French. Their vernacular Bible, and Chaucer's own, was the *Bible historiale complétée.*[65] Langland (*ob. c.* 1400), more overtly serious, quotes the Bible extensively in Latin.[66] But there is no clear evidence that in the later fourteenth century the English intelligentsia read, or English patrons commissioned,[67] an English Bible as such. The Wycliffite Bible (**no. 23**) is thus an academic exercise. The limits to its circulation and ultimate influence may be attributed not only to Archbishop Arundel's penal legislation of 1407, but to the absence of a wider social context in which it could be used. Professor Hudson's phrase, 'the premature reformation',[68] applies equally to the Wycliffite Bible itself—it was a translation before its time. A century and more was to pass before the English Bible would reach maturity in the hands of William Tyndale.[69]

Books of Hours

Common ground for the devout laity, and clergy, of the fourteenth and fifteenth centuries was attendance at Mass, the provision of Masses for others and the domestic devotion of the Book of Hours (**no. 22**). Although the ultimate source of the Book of Hours is the monastic office, and thus essentially the Psalter, the visual focus is more complex, including the Life of the Virgin, the Passion of Christ, the memorials of a relatively small group of favorite saints and the Office of the Dead. The verbal correlative of this familiar iconography is the equally familiar texts of Psalter and liturgy. Books of Hours needed no translation. Their appearance in French, Dutch and English in the late fifteenth century indicates the improved status of the vernacular rather than any need to translate 'Deus in adiutorium meum intende'. Like the 'Paris Bibles' (**no. 19**),

---

[62]The fundamental study is S. Berger, *La Bible française au Moyen Age* (Paris, 1884), pp. 109–156. Renaissance editions of this and other French Bibles are listed by B. T. Chambers, *Bibliography of French Bibles: Fifteenth- and Sixteenth-Century French Language Editions of the Scriptures* (Geneva, 1983). See C. R. Sneddon, 'The "Bible du XIIIe siècle": Its Medieval Public in the Light of Its Manuscript Tradition' in *The Bible and Medieval Culture,* ed. W. Lourdaux and D. Verhelst (Leuven, 1979), pp. 127–40. For a recent *mise-au-point* see G. Hasenohr, 'Bibles et psautiers' in *Mise en page,* pp. 317–27, at p. 323.

[63]It is easily assumed that 'the Church' opposed vernacular translation, *tout court.* But Innocent III, who is often quoted in this respect, condemned disobedience to canon law, rather than translation as such, or its use: L. E. Boyle, 'Innocent III and Vernacular Versions of Scripture', in *The Bible in the Medieval World: Essays in Memory of Beryl Smalley,* ed. K. Walsh and D. Wood, Studies in Church History, Subsidia 4 (Oxford, 1985), pp. 97–107.

[64]Sc. the new commentary of the eleventh and twelfth centuries as presented by Peter Comestor, rather than the patristic commentary to be found in the *Glossa ordinaria.*

[65]For Chaucer's knowledge of the *Bible historiale complétée* see D. R. Johnson, 'The Biblical Characters of Chaucer's Monk', *Publications of the Modern Language Society of America* 66 (1951) 827–43 (I am indebted for this reference to Helen Cooper).

[66]See further J. A. Alford, 'The Role of the Quotations in *Piers Plowman*', *Speculum* 52 (1977) 80–99.

[67]R. Hanna, 'Sir Thomas Berkeley and His Patronage', *Speculum* 64 (1989) 878–916.

[68]A. Hudson, *The Premature Reformation: Wycliffite Texts and Lollard History* (Oxford, 1988), chap. 5.

[69]S. L. Greenslade, 'English Versions of the Bible, 1525–1611' in *The Cambridge History of the Bible, 3: The West from the Reformation to the Present Day,* ed. S. L. Greenslade (Cambridge, 1963), pp. 141–47. Note that Tyndale was normally translating from the Hebrew and Greek.

Books of Hours were produced in quantity by experienced stationers for an assured market. It was the soundest of all medieval publishing ventures—until the Reformation.

G. THE BIBLE IN PRINT

The New Technology

In the autumn of 1454 Aeneas Silvius Piccolomini, the future Pope Pius II, attended the imperial Reichstag at Frankfurt, whence he made an excursion down the river to Mainz.[70] There he visited Gutenberg's workshop and saw the *editio princeps* of the Vulgate Bible (**no. 25**). He marvelled at the quality of the print—mundissime ac correctissime littere, nulla in parte mendaces (beautifully legible and without errors and omissions)—and at the scale of the operation. At least one hundred and fifty Bibles had already been produced; buyers were queuing up.[71] By 1454 the technical snags had been eliminated, so completely that not a trace survives of such initial experiments and failures as there may have been. Movable-type printing might not always be the cheapest and most convenient form of reproduction—witness the alternative technology of the block-books (**no. 24**)—but from the 1450s it was a fully available option in the cities of the middle and upper Rhine.

Printing and Publishing

Printing is only half the battle, or even less. The issues of the next century were threefold: the establishment of a 'good' text, permission to print that text, and its effective distribution. The correspondence of the early printers is full of deals, counter-deals and accusations of skullduggery. A papal or episcopal privilege was permission to print, but—far more important—it was protection against a rival printing of the same text in a way better adjusted to a still limited market. The Venice edition of the *Glossed Bible* with Nicholas of Lyra (**no. 16**), which invoked curial patronage but had no formal privilege to inhibit competition, was trumped three years later by Froben of Basel. But these are battles long ago; what interests the reader of today is the quality of the text.

The Authoritative Text

The ambitions and the achievement of biblical scholars in the later fifteenth and early sixteenth centuries varied according to the language with which they were concerned. Although they were very sensitive to Latin style and were beginning to explore textual criticism, they had no hope of establishing a valid critical edition of the Vulgate.[72] It was one thing to compare the Verona and Worms manuscripts of Livy, or to invoke a third witness, newly discovered in Speyer.[73] But manuscripts of the Vulgate were legion, and the fifteenth-century text the product of a millennium

---

[70]E. Meuthen, 'Ein neues frühes Quellenzeugnis (zu Oktober 1454?) für den ältesten Bibeldruck', *Gutenberg Jahrbuch* 57 (1982) 108–118, at p. 110.

[71]In the words of Aeneas Silvius's letter: 'antequam perficerentur volumina, paratos emptores fuisse tradunt' (Meuthen, 'Quellenzeugnis', p. 110).

[72]The pioneering work was Lorenzo Valla's *Collatio Novi Testamenti* (1442/43), the second redaction of which (1453/57) was published by Erasmus in 1505. See J. H. Bentley, *The Humanists and Holy Writ: New Testament Scholarship in the Renaissance* (Princeton, 1983), chap. 2. The first redaction is edited by A. Perosa, *Lorenzo Valla, Collatio Novi Testamenti* (Florence, 1970) and the second by E. Garin, *Valla, Opera omnia* (Turin, 1962) 1.801–895.

[73]See the prologues to the 1535 edition of Livy, by Beatus Rhenanus and Sigismund Gelenius for Froben of Basel; cf. L. D. Reynolds, 'Livy' in *Texts and Transmission: A Survey of the Latin Classics,* ed. L. D. Reynolds (Oxford, 1983), pp. 205–214.

of corruption and revision. The better course might be to make a new Latin translation from the original tongues. Cardinal Ximenes provided the Vulgate and the Septuagint in parallel to the Hebrew (**no. 27**), but in general the best that could be expected was a Latin version of the Septuagint. Erasmus made a complete translation of the New Testament from the original Greek (**no. 26**).

At the same time the Latin Bible as such was of uncertain status. Either the scholar read the sacred text in the original, or the plain man read a vernacular translation, which he recognized to be at one remove from that original. Luther's German Bible was for congregational devotion; theologians were expected to consult the original. By the mid-sixteenth century serious scholars did know Greek. Even Hebrew was coming to be taught at university: lectureships were established in Louvain (*c.* 1517), Paris (1530), Cambridge (1535) and Oxford (*c.* 1542).[74] What saved the Latin Bible was the Council of Trent, the fourth session of which (1546) was devoted to the canon and authority of the 'uetus uulgata latina editio', the elimination of other Latin versions and—so far as possible—the control of random and anonymous printed editions. The Vulgate was confirmed as the basis of preaching, teaching and study.[75]

By the word of the Lord were the heavens made (Ps. 33:6).

The men and women who commissioned and wrote these manuscripts of the Bible—patrons, scribes, annotators and expositors—all shared the assumption that the word of the Lord was the life-force in the material world. When the prophet spoke, the dry bones that lay scattered across the valley half-embedded in the soil reassembled themselves, not as skeletons but as living people.

> So I prophesied as he commanded me, and the breath came into them and they lived, and stood up upon their feet, an exceeding great army (Ezek. 37:10).

How did they regard the text and its variants? Was the text literally inspired? If not, could it be the word of God? If so, could it bear translation? Should we not all learn Hebrew and Greek? In an Islamic society these are not idle questions even today. But the view taken in the medieval west seems generally to have been robustly practical. That the Bible is the word of God neither inhibits nor absolves us from emending a corrupt reading against a better one. Indeed such a critical spirit is best shown in respect of the Bible, as the text *par excellence* that we need to understand.

---

[74]See P. S. Allen, 'The Trilingual Colleges of the Early Sixteenth Century' in *Erasmus: Lectures and Wayfaring Sketches* (Oxford, 1934), pp. 138–63.

[75]S. Kuttner, *Decreta septem priorum sessionum Concilii tridentini sub Paulo III Pont. Max.* (Washington, 1945), pp. 18–27.

LIST OF PLATES

A. LATE ANTIQUITY

B. THE CAROLINGIANS

C. VERNACULAR BIBLES

D. MONASTIC BIBLES

16. The 'Glossa Ordinaria' with Nicholas of Lyra, printed in Venice 1495: Oxford, Bodleian Library, Auct. V.Q.inf.II.6, fol. 279r.

E. THE UNIVERSITY TEXT

17. Peter Lombard, 'Magna Glosatura' on the Pauline Epistles: Oxford, Bodleian Library, MS Bodley 725, fol. 10r.

18. Stephen Langton, Commentary on Ruth: Oxford, Bodleian Library, MS Rawl. C. 427, fol. 66v.

19. The 'Paris Bible': Princeton, N.J., William H. Scheide Library, MS Scheide 7, fol. 298v.

20. A Hebrew-Latin Psalter: Leiden, Bibliotheek der Rijksuniversiteit, MS Scaliger Hebr. 8, fol. 5r.

F. THE NEW LITERACY

21. *La Bible historiale complétée:* London, British Library, MS Royal 17.E.VII, vol. 1, fol. 9r.

22. A Book of Hours: Notre Dame, Ind., University of Notre Dame, University Libraries, MS 4, fols. 135v–136r.

23. The Wycliffite Bible: Oxford, Christ Church, MS 145, fol. 232r.

24. The Block-Book Apocalypse: Oxford, Bodleian Library, Auct. M.IV.15, p. 21.

G. THE BIBLE IN PRINT

25. Gutenberg's Bible, printed in Mainz 1453–55: Oxford, Bodleian Library, Arch. B.b.10–11 (not foliated).

26. Erasmus's Translation of Luke and John: London, British Library, MS Royal 1.E.V, Part II, fol. 205v.

27. The Complutensian Polyglot: Princeton, N.J., William H. Scheide Library, 8.2.9.

28. Luther's 'Septembertestament': London, British Library, C.36.g.7, fol. lxix$^{v'}$.

A. LATE ANTIQUITY

1. The Tours Pentateuch: Paris, Bibliothèque Nationale, MS nouv. acq. lat. 2334, fol. 127v. s. vi/vii: North Africa or Spain.

A page from the Tours (or Ashburnham) Pentateuch, the earliest extant manuscript of the Latin text of Genesis-Leviticus; only the *capitula* survive to Deuteronomy, the fifth book of Moses.

Parchment; iv + 142 + iii fol.; quires of eight; page 375 x 310 mm.; text 280 x 238 mm.; 28/29 lines. The page, pricked down the center, was ruled and written before being illuminated. The square format is characteristic of a late antique manuscript.

Numbers 11.16–20. The textual affiliation is with cathedral manuscripts of Spain (Quentin, 1926, pp. xii–xx, 137). The text has been verified by a contemporary corrector (here audi*ui:* col. 1), whose 'contuli ut potui' survives at the end of Genesis (fol. 49v) and Leviticus (fol. 115r). It is in double columns throughout, with offset capitals and frequent section-headings in red (fol. 12v onwards: see Weitzmann, pl. 46). Several scribes may be identified, all mediocre. They are not illegible or incompetent or careless; but visually their work lacks elegance and beauty of line. The manuscript has seventeen major illuminations (the title page, ten to Genesis, five to Exodus, none to Leviticus, and one, here shown, to Numbers), and prefatory lists of *capitula* within 'canon-table' arches (cf. **no. 5** below) to Exodus, Numbers and Deuteronomy. The *capitula* for Genesis and Leviticus are lost, but the title-page for the whole volume is painted in good-quality rustic capitals (fol. 2r). The full-page pictures are carefully inscribed in white (as here) or gold minuscule. Here the spirit of Moses is conveyed to the seventy elders who will serve the Tabernacle (above left and below) and govern the people (above right).

In the mid-eighth century the book was refurbished in a *scriptorium* in eastern France, possibly Fleury (cf. Lowe, 1.93). These replacement leaves, repairs (e.g. fol. 43v) and corrections (e.g. here col. 2: 'reppuleritis dn̄m̄ qui'; Weitzmann, pl. 46, col. 1 to*llens*) are a silent condemnation of the original script. Now the ink is black, the pen sharp and the strokes firm. It is a fine example of an insular technique, still in touch with the tradition of antique uncial. Fifty years later in Tours, another missing page was supplied (fol. 33r) and omissions noted in Tironian shorthand: 'd-7 [sc. deest] folium 1' (fol. 126v and elsewhere). The erasure of the Second Person of the Trinity in the Creation miniature (fol. 1v: Narkiss, 1969, pp. 46–52) was perhaps also the work of a 'corrector' at Tours, aware of Alcuin's hostility to Adoptionism (Cavadini). The pictures may have served as prototypes for some illumination in the Tours Bibles of *c.* 820–50 (Kessler, p. 142); more remarkably they were a model for the series of eleventh-century frescoes in the nave of St. Julien, Tours (Grabar).

The book seems to have remained in Tours until 1843, when Libri acquired it from the Bibliothèque Municipale and sold it to Lord Ashburnham. By the tenacity of Léopold Delisle it returned in 1885 to France: to the Bibliothèque Nationale and not (as Delisle insisted) to its improvident custodians in Tours.

Bibliography: Cahn [excellent plate of fol. 76r]; J. C. Cavadini, *The Last Christology of the West: Adoptionism in Spain and Gaul 785–820* (Philadelphia, 1993); Y. Christe (*Cahiers archéologiques* [1990], 7–16), inferring the existence of another, similar illustrated Pentateuch; Fischer, 'Alkuin-Bibeln', pp. 349–57; O. von Gebhardt, *The Miniatures of the Ashburnham Pentateuch* (London, 1883); A. Grabar, 'Fresques romanes copiés sur les miniatures du Pentateuch de Tours', *Cahiers archéologiques* 9 (1957) 329–41; H. L. Kessler, *The Illustrated Bibles from Tours* (Princeton, 1977); Lowe, *CLA* 693a–b; B. Narkiss, 'Towards a Further Study of the Ashburnham Pentateuch (Pentateuch de Tours)', *Cahiers archéologiques* 19 (1969) 45–60; 22 (1972), 19–38; F. Rickert, *Studien zum Ashburnham Pentateuch* (Doctoral Dissertation; Bonn, 1986); K. Weitzmann, *Late Antique and Early Christian Book Illumination* (London, 1977), no. XIV, pll. 44–47 and pp. 22–24.

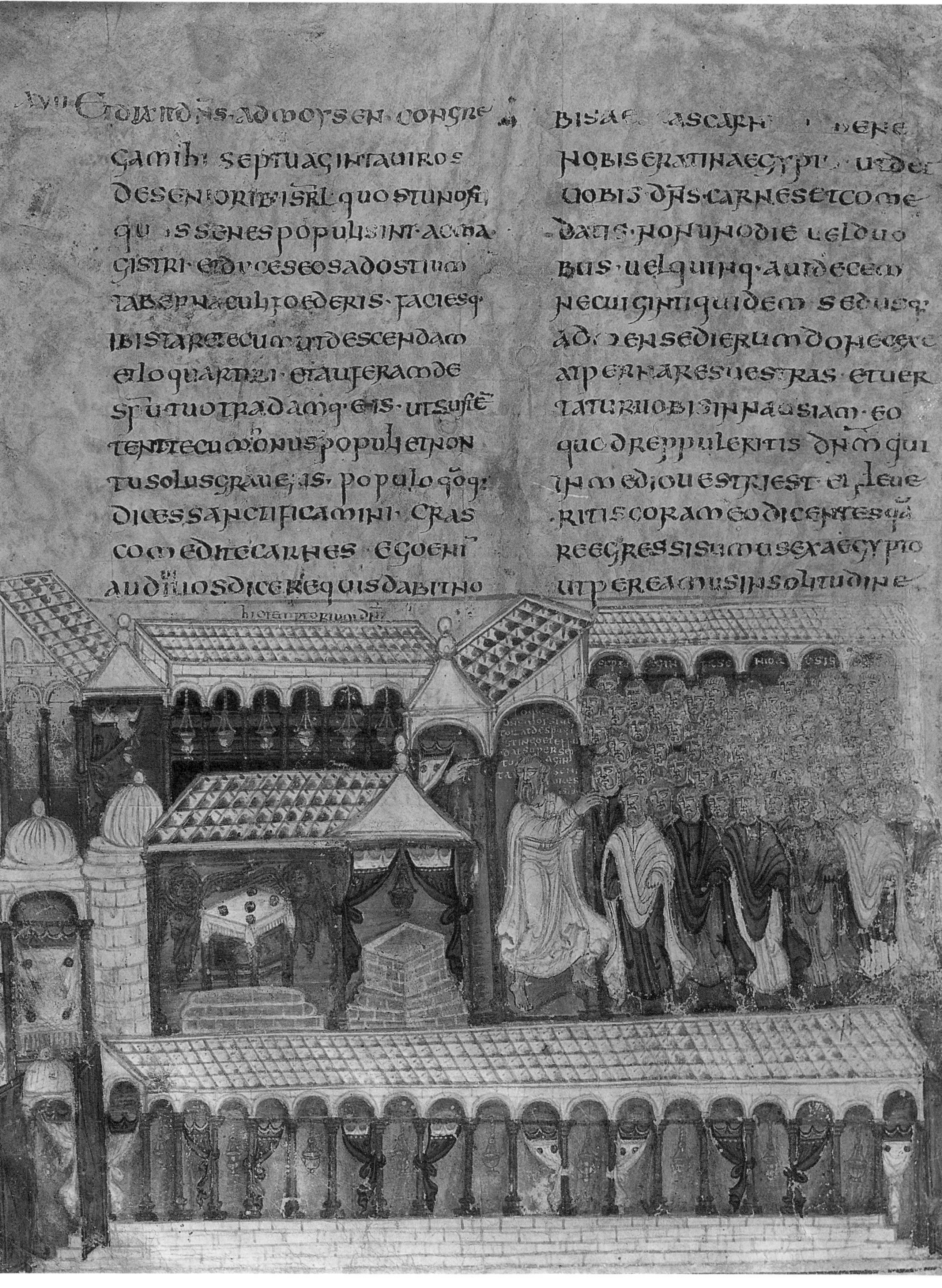

XVII Et dixit dns ad moysen congre-
ga mihi septuaginta uiros
de senioribus isrl quos tu nosti
quod senes populi sint ac ma-
gistri et duc eseos ad ostium
tabernaculi foederis faciesq·
ibi stare tecum ut descendam
et loquar tibi et auferam de
spu tuo tradamq· eis ut suste-
tent tecum onus populi et non
tu solus graueris populo quoq·
dices sanctificamini cras
comedite carnes ego enī
audiui uos dicere quis dabit no-

bis esc[illegible] carn[illegible] bene
nobis erat in aegypto ut det
uobis dns carnes et come-
datis non uno die uel duobus uel quinq· aut decem
nec uiginti quidem sed usq·
ad mensem dierum donec exe-
at per nares uestras et uer-
tatur uobis in nausiam eo
quod reppuleritis dnm qui
in medio uestri est et fleue-
ritis coram eo dicentes quā-
re egressi sumus ex aegypto
ut pereamus in solitudine

2. The Laudian Acts: Oxford, Bodleian Library, MS Laud Graec. 35, fol. 77r. s. vi/vii: ?Sardinia.

The Acts of the Apostles in Greek with the 'Vetus latina' translation in parallel. As the Greek text supplied Bede with over seventy readings, many unique, for his *Retractatio* on Acts (Metzger, note 2), it is difficult to resist the inference that this very manuscript was in his hands in about 720. Here Bede notes the reading, 'When *Paul* came into Jerusalem' (lines 10–11), which preempts Saul's change of name to Paul (*Retractatio* 9.26; ed. Laistner, pp. 137–38).

Parchment; 227 fol.; page 268 x 206 mm.; text 200 x 178 mm.; col. 200 x 78 mm.; 25 lines; single vertical boundary-lines to each column. Written by a Greek scribe, who has adjusted some Latin letter-forms to his own practice (Lowe).

The scribe seems to be working from a Latin exemplar, to which he adds the Greek equivalent line-for-line. That he sometimes repeats a line at the top of a new page (Metzger) suggests that this is his original draft: a one-off correlation of unfamiliar Latin with familiar Greek. The cramped lines 2 and 10 (both adding *autem,* Gk δὲ) similarly indicate that this is a working transcript rather than a fair copy.

As to where the manuscript was written, and for whom, we can say only that it belongs to a Greek-speaking milieu in which Latin was studied as a second language. Current scholarly opinion favors an unidentified monastery in southern Italy or Sardinia, but only on the very general grounds that this was the sort of text that a monk would read. The first serious indication of provenance is on the end flyleaf, which contains a fragmentary document in Greek (post-534: Metzger) referring to Sardinia; but when the flyleaf was put to its present use we do not know. Bede's many quotations indicate that this manuscript, or its twin, had reached England by the early eighth century; only the absence of Anglo-Saxon annotation inhibits the hypothesis that it was acquired by Benedict Biscop in Rome and presented by him to Monkwearmouth-Jarrow.

Eventually Archbishop Laud was to acquire the manuscript at Würzburg in 1633 and present it to the Bodleian Library. How long it had been in Würzburg is quite uncertain—perhaps already in support of the Anglo-Saxon missions in the eighth century, perhaps much later. The identification in the cathedral book-lists of *c.* 800 and *c.* 1000 (Knaus, pp. 979 and 985) essentially depends on the manuscript's presence in Würzburg about 1630.

Bibliography: *Bedae Venerabilis Expositio Actuum Apostolorum et Retractatio,* ed. M. L. W. Laistner (Cambridge, Mass., 1939; rpt. CCSL 121, Turnhout, 1983); H. O. Coxe, *Bodleian Library Quarto Catalogues, II: Laudian Manuscripts,* rev. R. W. Hunt (Oxford, 1973); H. Knaus, *Bistum Würzburg* (Mittelalterliche Bibliothekskataloge Deutschlands und der Schweiz, 4.2; Munich, 1979), pp. 977–88; Lowe, *CLA,* no. 251: B. M. Metzger, *Manuscripts of the Greek Bible: An Introduction to Palaeography* (Oxford, 1981), no. 22 [an excellent critique with further bibliography].

	OCCIDERENT	ΑΝΕΛΩϹΙΝ
	ACCEPTUMAUTEM	ΛΑΒΟΝΤΕϹΔΕ
	EUM	ΑΥΤΟΝ
	DISCIPULI	ΟΙΜΑΘΗΤΑΙ
	NOCTE	ΝΥΚΤΟϹ
	PERMURUM	ΔΙΑΤΟΥΤΙΧΟΥϹ
	DIMISERUNT	ΚΑΘΗΚΑΝ
	LAXANTES	ΧΑΛΑϹΑΝΤΕϹ
	INSPORTA	ΕΝϹΠΥΡΙΔΙ
	CUMUENISSETAUTEM	ΠΑΡΑΓΕΝΟΜΕΝΟϹΔΕ
	PAULUS	ΟΠΑΥΛΟϹ
	INHIEROSOLYMIS	ΕΝΙΛΗΜ
	TEMPTABAT	ΕΠΕΙΡΑΤΟ
	ADHAERERE	ΚΟΛΛΑϹΘΑΙ
	DISCIPULIS	ΤΟΙϹΜΑΘΗΤΑΙϹ
	ETOMNES	ΚΑΙΠΑΝΤΕϹ
	TIMEBANT	ΕΦΟΒΟΥΝΤΟ
	EUM	ΑΥΤΟΝ
	NONCREDENTES	ΜΗΠΙϹΤΕΥΟΝΤΕϹ
	QUOD	ΟΤΙ
	EST	ΕϹΤΙΝ
	DISCIPULUS	ΜΑΘΗΤΗϹ
CX II.	BARNABASAUTEM	ΒΑΡΝΑΒΑϹΔΕ
	ADSUMENS	ΕΠΙΛΑΒΟΜΕΝΟϹ
	EUM	ΑΥΤΟΝ
	ADDUXIT	ΗΓΑΓΕΝ

3. A Ceolfrid Bible: London, British Library, MS Loan 81 ('The Bankes Leaf'), recto. *c.* 680: Monkwearmouth-Jarrow.

A leaf of one of the three great Bibles written in Monkwearmouth-Jarrow at the direction of Ceolfrid, who later became abbot of the twin houses (689–716). One of these Bibles survives complete: sent as a gift to Pope Gregory II, and now the *Codex Amiatinus* in the Laurenziana Library in Florence. Eleven folios survive of the second: London, British Library, MSS Add. 45025 (= fragments of III-IV Kings) + Add. 37777 (= III Kings 11:29–12:18). The Bankes Leaf may well be the only extant witness to the third (= Ecclesiasticus 35:10–37:2).[1]

Parchment; a disjoint leaf: page 413 x 332 mm.; text 364 x 254 mm.; column 364 x 119 mm.; letters 4 mm. high; 44 lines. Horizontal ruling only, with pricking in the inner and outer margins. The absence of vertical ruling distinguishes this leaf from both *Amiatinus* and the other fragments in the British Library (figure in Petitmengin, *Amiatinus,* p. 74). The script is a fine, square uncial with hair-line descenders to **g** and hair-line decoration of **a**. There is no punctuation, and infrequent word-division. But the text as a whole is deployed in units of meaning. These may be more than a sentence and less than, or different from, the verses of Scripture familiar today. A unit, which is marked by two letters offset to the left (e.g. *SE*D IUDICABIT: col. 2, line 1), has one major pause and a clearly defined ending. Such a disposition *per cola et commata* (both words meaning a syntactical phrase or unit of meaning) originated in antique rhetorical texts as an aid to public declamation. It became a familiar feature of the Bible text only in Jerome's Vulgate (Petitmengin, 'Les plus anciens manuscrits', pp. 103–105). Another such guide is the rhetorical heading, DEPRECATIO AD DEVM (col. 2, line 18, in red), 'addressing a petition to God'. Chapter-divisions (cf. **no. 18**) were added in the thirteenth or fourteenth century: an offset red paraph sign with a Roman numeral and red highlighting of the first line of each new chapter.

Bede records when and how these great Bibles were written. Having visited Rome with his abbot, Benedict Biscop, in 678, Ceolfrid himself 'added three pandects of the new translation to the one of the old translation which he had brought from Rome'.[2] In their spacious two-column format and in their uncial script, *Amiatinus* and the fragments reflect a Roman 'codex grandior' (cf. Cassiodorus, *Inst.* 1.14.2). The Esdras frontispiece, the canon-tables and the drawings in *Amiatinus* are in the same tradition. The deployment *per cola et commata* however has been borrowed from Jerome's Vulgate; and the text itself is the Vulgate rather than Jerome's revision of the Hexapla, which Cassiodorus thought appropriate to a 'codex grandior'. In Bede's language, Ceolfrid's three Bibles were modeled visually on the 'vetus translatio', modified by the deployment *per cola et commata,* but textually on the 'noua translatio' (cf. Cassiodorus, *Inst.* 1.12.3).

Bibliography: *Cassiodori senatoris Institutiones,* ed. R. A. B. Mynors (Oxford, 1937); Bede, *Historia abbatum,* ed. C. Plummer, *Historia ecclesiastica,* 2 vols. (Oxford, 1896) 1.364–87. J. J. G. Alexander, *Insular Manuscripts: 6th to the 9th Century* (A Survey of Manuscripts Illuminated in the British Isles, 1; London, 1978), no. 7 (*Amiatinus*); Fischer, *Amiatinus;* Lowe *CLA* 177 (British Library Add. 37777 and 45025) and *CLA* 299 (*Amiatinus*); E. A. Lowe, *English Uncial* (Oxford, 1960), nos. VIII-IX (*Amiatinus*) and X (Ceolfrid fragments); M. B. Parkes, *The Scriptorium of Wearmouth-Jarrow* (Jarrow Lecture, 1982; Jarrow-on-Tyne, 1982); Petitmengin, 'Les plus anciens manuscrits', pp. 89–127; *Amiatinus,* pp. 72–77; L. Webster and J. Backhouse, *The Making of England: Anglo-Saxon Art and Culture, AD 600–900* (A British Museum and British Library Exhibition Catalogue; London, 1991), no. 87, pp. 122-23.

[1]See Introduction, p. 4.

[2]'Tres pandectes nouae translationis, ad unum vetustae translationis quem de Roma adtulerat, ipse super adiungeret' (*Historia abbatum,* p. 379).

ET NON MINUAS PRIMITIAS
MANUUM TUARUM
IN OMNI DATO HILAREM
FAC UULTUM TUUM
ET IN EXULTATIONE SCIFICA
DECIMAS TUAS
DA ALTISSIMO SECUNDUM
DATUM EIUS
ET IN BONO OCULO ADINUENTIONĒ
FAC MANUUM TUARUM
QUONIAM DNS RETRIBUENS EST
ET SEPTIES TANTO REDDET TIBI
NOLI OFFERRE MUNERA PRAUA
NON ENIM SUSCIPIET ILLA
ET NOLI INSPICERE SACRIFICIUM
INIUSTUM
QUONIAM DNS IUDEX EST ET NON
EST APUD ILLUM GLORIA
PERSONAE
NON ACCIPIET DNS PERSONAM
IN PAUPEREM
ET PRAECATIONEM LAESI EXAUDIET
NON DISPICIET PRAECES PUPILLI
NEC UIDUAM SI EFFUNDAT
LOQUELLAM GEMITUS
NON NE LACRIMAE UIDUAE
AD MAXILLAM DESCENDUNT
EXCLAMATIO EIUS SUPER
DEDUCENTEM EAS
A MAXILLA ENIM ASCENDUNT
USQUE AD CAELUM
ET DNS EXAUDITOR NON DELEC
TABITUR IN ILLIS
QUI ADORAT DM IN OBLECTATIONE
SUSCIPIETUR
ET PRAECATIO ILLIUS USQUE
AD NUBES PROPINQUAUIT
ORATIO HUMILIANTIS
SE NUBES PENETRAUIT
ET DONEC PROPINQUET
NON CONSOLABITUR
ET NON DISCEDIT DONEC
ASPICIAT ALTISSIMUS
ET DNS NON ELONGAUIT

SED IUDICABIT IUSTO ET FACIET
IUDICIUM
ET FORTISSIMUS NON HABEBIT
IN ILLIS PATIENTIAM
UT CONTRIBULET DORSUM IPSORŪ
ET GENTIBUS REDDET UINDICTĀ
DONEC TOLLAT PLENITUDINEM
SUPERBORUM ET SCEPTRA
INIQUORUM CONTRIBULET
DONEC REDDAT HOMINIBUS
SECUNDUM ACTUS SUOS
ET SECUNDUM OPERA ADAE
ET SECUNDUM PRAESUMPTIONĒ ILLIU
DONEC IUDICET IUDICIUM
PLEBIS SUAE
ET OBLECTAUIT IUSTOS
MISERICORDIA SUA
DEPRAECATIO AD DM
SPECIOSA MISERICORDIA DI
IN TEMPORE TRIBULATIONIS
QUASI NUBES PLUUIAE
IN TEMPORE SICCITATIS
MISERERE NOSTRI DS
OMNIUM ET RESPICE NOS
ET OSTENDE NOBIS LUCEM
MISERATIONUM TUARUM
ET IMMITTE TIMOREM TUUM
SUPER GENTES QUAE NON
EXQUISIERUNT TE
ET COGNOSCANT QUIA NON EST DS
NISI TU UT ENARRENT
MAGNALIA TUA
ALLEUA MANUM TUAM SUPER
GENTES ALIENAS UT UIDEANT
POTENTIAM TUAM
SICUT ENIM IN CONSPECTU EORŪ
SCIFICATUS ES IN NOBIS
SIC IN CONSPECTU NOSTRO
MAGNIFICAUERIS IN ILLIS
K UT COGNOSCANT TE SICUT
ET NOS AGNOUIMUS
QUONIAM NON EST DS PRAETER
TE DNE
INNOUA SIGNA ET IMMUTA MIRABILIA

4. The Lindisfarne Gospels with the Stonyhurst Gospel of St. John: London, British Library, MSS Cotton Nero D.IV, fol. 234v and Loan 74, fol. 46v. both s. vii4/4: Lindisfarne.

A page of St. John's Gospel in a grand insular folio and a minuscule pocket gospelbook. *Lindisfarne* is prodigal of space, having only 148 words (John 10:9–18) as against the 80 words (John 10:8–13) on the tiny page of *Stonyhurst.*

Lindisfarne: page 340 x 250 mm.; text 235 x 190 mm.; column 235 x 85 mm.; 24 lines; each page ruled individually (Ker, no. 165). Written *per cola et commata* in insular majuscule, having rarely more than three words per line, with small decorated initials marking the *capitula,* the Ammonian sections and occasionally elsewhere (Facsimile, pp. 80–81: Brown). An interlinear gloss in Anglo-Saxon minuscule was added in the later tenth century (Ker, McGurk). Sixteen pages of canon-tables (fol. 10r–17v); an Evangelist-portrait, a carpet-page and a major initial preceding each Gospel (Alexander, no. 9).

Stonyhurst: page 135 x 90 mm.; text 92 x 61 mm.; 19 lines (to fol. 42v), 20 lines (fol. 43r–90v), having two vertical boundary-columns (about 4 mm.) on each side of the text. Written *per cola et commata* in 'capitular uncial' (Lowe), with red initials marking the 45 *capitula* and black initials the Ammonian sections (Brown, *Stonyhurst,* p. 24: here 'Ego', line 11, begins a *capitulum*). The manuscript is in its original binding of red goatskin on birchwood, with a deep relief of fruit and leaves on the front cover. No comparable binding survives.

Both manuscripts were written for (it is widely assumed) the community of Lindisfarne between 675 and 700. Cuthbert had been prior there for a decade, and later bishop. He was regarded as a saint in his lifetime; the cult intensified after his death in 687. In 698 his uncorrupt body was brought into the monastic church. There the saint lay with *Stonyhurst* by his hand, in a wooden coffin incised with drawings of Christ and the Virgin, the archangels and the apostles (Battiscombe). In the context of this cult *Lindisfarne* was sumptuously bound, and the binding inlaid with gemstones and gold (colophon, fol. 259r: see Facsimile, 2 [text], pp. 5–10). The cult continued through the eighth century, beyond the catastrophe of 793, when the Vikings sacked Lindisfarne. They did not destroy the community. The 'congregation of St. Cuthbert' (Craster) gathered up the saint in his coffin, the gospelbook and such other treasures as could be transported, and set out itinerant across northern England: toward Carlisle (875), back to Chester-le-Street (883) and eventually in 995 to Durham. There St. Cuthbert rested, with *Stonyhurst* in his coffin and *Lindisfarne* on his altar. When finally the sixteenth-century reformers destroyed the cult, the coffin and its contents were spirited away by the local Catholics—the coffin to return to Durham itself and *Stonyhurst* to be preserved in the Jesuit college in Lancashire from which it takes its name.

Bibliography: Facsimile, T. J. Brown, R. L. S. Bruce-Mitford et al., *Codex Lindisfarnensis,* 2 vols. (Oltun and Lausanne, 1960); J. Backhouse, *The Lindisfarne Gospels* (Oxford, 1981); T. J. Brown, *The Stonyhurst Gospel of St. John* (Roxburghe Club, Oxford, 1969). J. J. G. Alexander, *Insular Manuscripts: 6th to the 9th Centuries* (A Survey of Manuscripts Illuminated in the British Isles, 1; London, 1978), no. 9; C. F. Battiscombe, *The Relics of Saint Cuthbert* (Oxford, 1956); G. Bonner, D. Rollason and C. Stancliffe, *St. Cuthbert, His Cult and His Community to AD 1200* (Woodbridge, 1989); T. J. Brown, 'Late Antique and Early Anglo-Saxon Books' in A. C. de la Mare and B. C. Barker-Benfield, *Manuscripts at Oxford: An Exhibition in Memory of Richard William Hunt* (Oxford, 1980), pp. 9–14; E. Craster, 'The Patrimony of St. Cuthbert', *English Historical Review* 69 (1954) 177–99; N. R. Ker, *Catalogue of Manuscripts Containing Anglo-Saxon* (Oxford, 1957); Lowe, *CLA* 187 (*Lindisfarne*) and 260 (*Stonyhurst*); E. A. Lowe, *English Uncial* (1960), no. VII; P. McGurk, *Latin Gospel Books from A.D. 400 to A.D. 800* (Les publications de *Scriptorium,* 5; Brussels/Amsterdam, 1961), nos. 22 (*Lindisfarne*) and 37 (*Stonyhurst*); Petitmengin, 'Les plus anciens manuscrits', pp. 95 and 112; Webster and Backhouse (as **no. 3**), nos. 80 (*Lindisfarne*) and 86 (*Stonyhurst*).

per me siquis introierit
saluabitur
et ingredietur
et egredietur
et pascua inueniet
fur non uenit nisi
ut furetur et mactet
et perdat
ego ueni ut uitam
habeant
et abundantius
habeant
Ego sum pastor bonus
bonus pastor animam

quia mercennarius est
et non pertinet ad eum
de ouibus
ego sum pastor bonus
et cognosco meas
et cognoscunt me meae
xc sicut nouit me pater
et ego agnosco patrem
xci et animam meam
pono pro ouib:
xcii et alias oues habeo
quae non sunt
ex hoc ouili
et illas oportet me
adducere
et uocem meam audient
et fiet unum ouile
unus pastor
propterea me
pater diligit
quia ego pono
animam meam
et iterum sumam eam
nemo tollit eam a me

sed non audierunt eos oues
ego sum ostium
per me siquis introierit
saluabitur
et ingredietur et egredietur
et pascua inueniet
fur non uenit nisi ut furetur
et mactet et perdat
ego ueni ut uitam habeant
et abundantius habeant
Ego sum pastor bonus
bonus pastor animam suam
dat pro ouibus
mercennarius et qui non est pastor
cuius non sunt oues propriae
uidet lupum uenientem
et dimittet oues et fugit
et lupus rapit et dispergit oues
mercennarius autem fugit
quia mercennarius est

B. THE CAROLINGIANS

5. Carolingian Canon-Tables: London, British Library, MS Harley 2795, fol. 11r. s. ix1/3.

Tables (κανόνες) showing where a section in one Gospel corresponds to the same material in another. For example Matthew ccxlviii [= 24:16–17] recurs at Mark cxliii [= 13:14–15] and Luke ccviii [= 17:31] and ccliii [= 21:21]. The same references are set in the margins of the text itself, in a microscopic hand; so the reader can turn directly from fol. 62r (Matthew) to fol. 104r (Mark) and the rest, without checking in the list at the beginning. This belt-and-braces approach is not unnecessary where so many Roman numerals are involved. Canon-tables were perhaps first developed in third-century Alexandria, when Ammonius divided Matthew into 355 'sections', and (it is conjectured) added in the margin references to the other three Gospels. Mark had about 235 sections, Luke about 343 and John about 232 (Vigouroux). The system was known to Origen, and further developed by Eusebius of Caesarea (*ob. c.* 340), historian and chronographer. Eusebius's contribution was to draw up ten tables correlating the 'sections' within each of the four Gospels: the first table based on Mark, the second—shown here—on Matthew, and so through eight further permutations. These tables were established in Greek, and contemporaneously in Syriac, gospelbooks; the Greek then acted as the model for Gothic and Latin. Carl Nordenfalk, whose indispensable analysis gives us security here, categorizes *Harley* as the 'shorter Latin' form. This has eight tables in all; in Harley 2795 two are missing. The page shown is from the second table: how Matthew's Gospel relates to the two other Synoptics. Our manuscript belongs in a group with seven others of the sixth to the ninth centuries. The same peacocks—little better drawn—are already at their posts in a manuscript from sixth-century Ravenna, and still present in a mid-eighth-century book that is now in Trier (Nordenfalk).

Measures: page 285 x 206 mm.; maximum height and width of arches 225 x 192 mm. The canon-tables are the sole formal decoration. Harley 2795 has no evangelist-portraits, and no elaborate initials: all the variety of color comes in the canon-tables. Otherwise the only concessions are the use of gold for the opening paragraph of each Gospel, red for the main text hand and—strikingly effective—the hierarchy and diversity of formal scripts at the beginning of each Gospel.

Harley 2795 was written in the Loire valley, and has long been associated with the great classical scholar, Lupus of Ferrières. *Se non è vero è ben trovato* is the best that we can say here. Lupus's hand is known (Beeson), and this is not it. His zeal to acquire manuscripts and his access to the products of the *scriptorium* of Tours are beyond question. Better perhaps to see Lupus as evidence of the intellectual climate of the upper Loire valley, to which Harley 2795 itself is an elegant witness.

Bibliography: C. H. Beeson, *Lupus of Ferrières as Scribe and Text Critic: A Study of His Autograph Copy of Cicero's De Oratore* (Cambridge, Mass., 1930); C. Nordenfalk, *Die spätantiken Kanontafeln,* 2 vols. (Die Buchornamentik der Spätantike, 1; Gothenburg, 1938); F. Vigouroux, *Dictionnaire de la Bible,* 5 vols. (Paris, 1891–1912) 1.493–94.

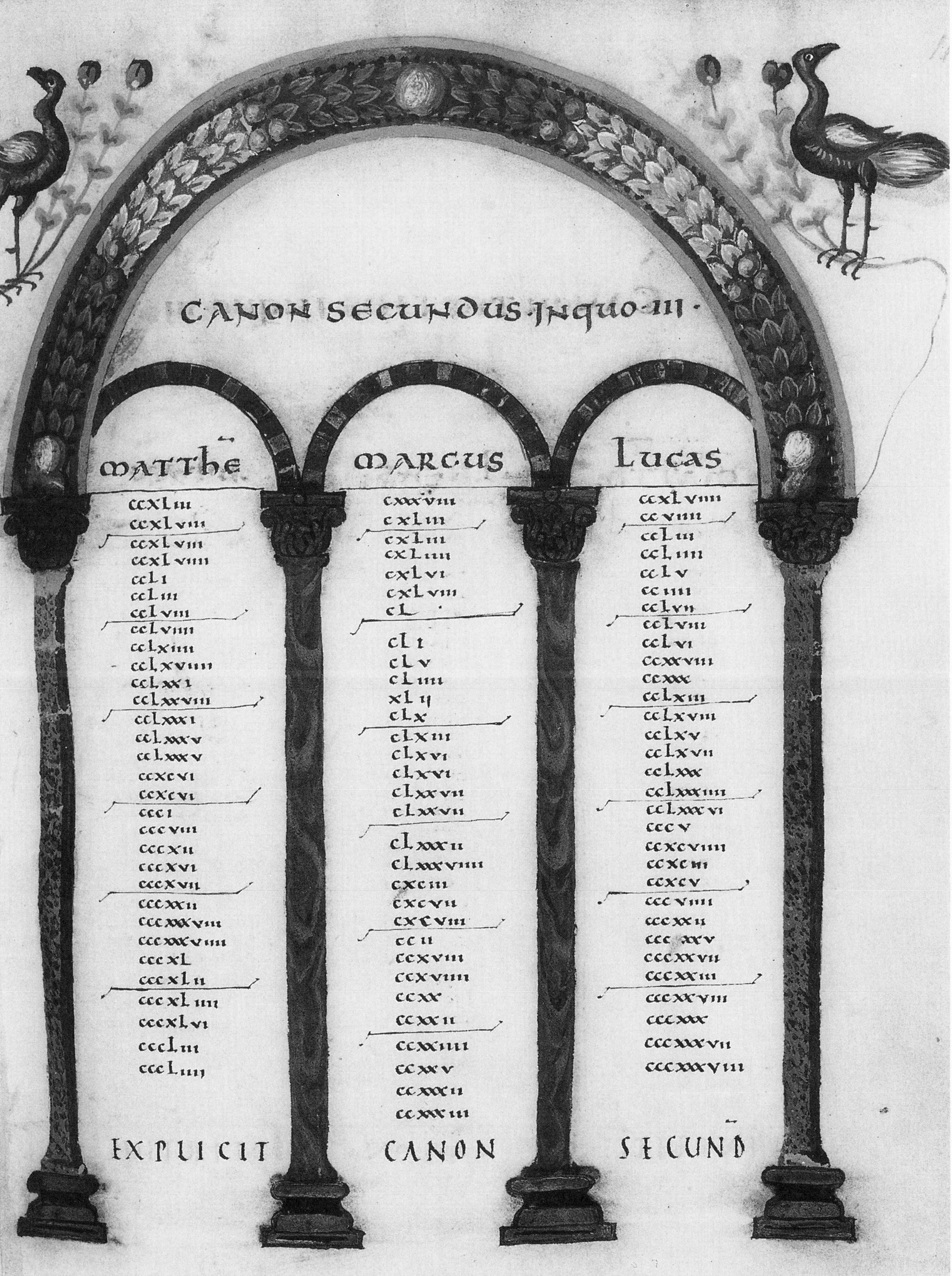

CANON SECUNDUS IN QUO III

MATTHE	MARCUS	LUCAS
ccxliii	cxxxviii	ccxlviiii
ccxlviii	cxliii	ccviiii
ccxlviii	cxliii	cclii
ccxlviiii	cxliiii	ccliiii
ccli	cxlvi	cclv
ccliii	cxlviii	cciiii
cclvii	cl	cclvii
cclviii	cli	cclviii
cclxiiii	clv	cclvi
cclxviiii	cliiii	ccxxviii
cclxxi	xlii	ccxxx
cclxxviii	clx	cclxiii
cclxxxi	clxiii	cclxviii
cclxxxv	clxvi	cclxv
cclxxxv	clxvi	cclxvii
ccxcvi	clxxvii	cclxxx
ccxcvi	clxxvii	cclxxxiiii
ccci	clxxxii	cclxxxvi
cccviii	clxxxviiii	cccv
cccxii	cxciii	ccxcviiii
cccxvi	cxcvii	ccxciii
cccxvii	cxcviii	ccxcv
cccxxii	ccii	cccviiii
cccxxxviii	ccxviii	cccxxii
cccxxxviiii	ccxviiii	ccc xxv
cccxl	ccxx	cccxxvii
cccxlii	ccxxii	cccxxiii
cccxliiii	ccxxiiii	cccxxviii
cccxlvi	ccxxv	cccxxx
cccliii	ccxxxii	cccxxxvii
cccliiii	ccxxxiii	cccxxxviii

EXPLICIT CANON SECUND

6. Theodulf's Text of the Bible: London, British Library, MS Add. 24142, fol. 57r. s. ix1/3: S. Hubert, Ardennes (dioc. Liège).

There are six Theodulf Bibles, and they are all different (Fischer, 'Bibeltext', pp. 135–47: Θ^{H}); each varies to some degree in the exemplars used for one part of the Bible or another. Theodulf acquires a new text of Job (let us say), and his next Bible incorporates that discovery. A Theodulf Bible was neither a presentation volume nor a service-book. Its 'fine print' would not always be legible in the uneven light of a liturgical ceremony. It was a book for the scholar to use in his study.

Parchment; iii + 248 + iii fol.; page 330 x 243 mm.; text 256 x 198 mm.; col. 256 x 62 mm.; tricolumnar; 62 lines. Double boundary-lines (2 mm. apart) on both sides of each column; the columns are 7 mm. apart. A number of scribes, all writing a minute hand such as would normally be used for gloss rather than text. No running titles in the upper margin. Canon-tables preceding the Gospels, but otherwise no decoration apart from a few colophons in display script. The manuscript is imperfect at the beginning and the end (*inc.* /in consilio eorum [Gen. 49:6], [*expl.* . . . ambulaverunt in/] [I Peter 4:3]).

Theodulf was interested in reconstructing a sound and ancient text of the Vulgate. It may indeed have been he who brought the Tours Pentateuch (**no. 1**) to the Loire valley.[1] He used the disposition *per cola et commata* for Job and the Wisdom-literature only: a distinction which predates Cassiodorus and may predate Jerome. His division of the Bible derives from Jerome and Cassiodorus:

<primus ordo legis>[2] [Genesis–Deuteronomy] fol. 1ra–31vb
secundus ordo prophetarum [Joshua–Hosea][3] fol. 31vc–109rb
tertius ordo agiographorum [Job–Esther] fol. 109rb–165vb
quartus ordo eorum librorum qui in veteri testamento extra canonem aebraeorum sunt
[Wisdom, Ecclesiasticus, Tobit, Judith, I–II Maccabees] fol. 165vb–196vc.

Another Cassiodoran trait is the word 'breues', used for the analytical 'capitula', or 'tituli' which precede the books of the Pentateuch and the books of history.[4] Some books, perhaps casually where space allowed, have their colophon in a vertical rectangle with simple foliage decoration at each corner: EXPLICIT MALACIM [sc. Kings]. INCIPIT LIBER ISAIE PROPH' (fol. 70v). The visual appearance of the colophon, rather than its content, is late antique. Finally we should notice (even if we do not explicate) the detailed cross-reference system of 'capitula' and marginal notes within the Pauline Epistles. This system was known to some Carolingian scholars via the *Diatessaron* of Victor of Capua (545/6), a manuscript that is believed to have belonged to St. Boniface.[5] But its origin is a good deal earlier, possibly in the circle of Pelagius (*ob.* 418+), and Theodulf could well have known it in other manuscripts, without recourse to Fulda.

Bibliography: Fischer, 'Bibelausgaben' and 'Bibeltext'; E. Ranke, *Codex Fuldensis* (Marburg/Leipzig, 1868) [= *Diatessaron*].

[1] In the Rome edition of the Vulgate the sigla are G (our **no. 1**) and Θ^{H} (our **no. 6**). To compare the two manuscripts in detail would be useful only within a comprehensive study of Theodulf's sources.

[2] As this Theodulf Bible is imperfect at the beginning, I have supplied the title from Paris, Bibliothèque Nationale, lat. 9380. For the first three orders see Cassiodorus, *Inst.* 1.12.1, quoting Jerome; cf. *Inst.* 1.1–9 *passim.*

[3] Joel–Malachi are missing.

[4] Petitmengin, 'Les plus anciens manuscrits', p. 102.

[5] Fischer, 'Bibelausgaben', pp. 57–66.

clxxvii Ubi zacharias rex iuda moritur et scriptura ad zachariam re
gem israhel redit
clxxviii Ubi zacharias occiditur et sellum pro eo in israhel regnum
suscepit et est xv rex finita promissione domini in impro
genies hieu
clxxviiii De occiso sellum qui regnauit mense uno pro quo manahen
suscepit regnum in israhel qui est xvi rex
clxxx Indicto argenti diuitibus manahen quod daretur regi syriae
clxxxi Ubi manahen moritur et regnat post eum phacea filius
eius et est xvii rex
clxxxii Ubi occiditur phacea a facee qui fuit rex xviii in israhel
clxxxiii Ubi osee filius phaceia occidit facee et regnauit xviiii in israhel
clxxxiiii Ubi scriptura redit ad ioatham regem iuda quem dicit regnasse annis xvi
clxxxv Ubi ioatham moritur et regnat achaz xii in iuda annis xvi
clxxxvi Ubi achaz rex iuda filium suum idolis consecrauit
clxxxvii Ubi achaz altare nouum fieri iubet ab uria sacerdote
clxxxviii Ubi ordinat rex achaz cum uria sacerdote quae sacrificia
noua altari inponantur
clxxxviiii Hic moritur achaz et regnat pro eo ezechias xiii
cxc Ubi redit scriptura ad regem israhel et ostendit osee reg
nasse viiii annis
cxci Hic explicit de regibus israhel qui fuerunt ab hieroboam usque in osee xviiii
captiuatur populus israhel a salmanasar rege assyriorum
cxcii De gentibus a rege assyriorum in samariam missis quae ducti
et a leonibus deuorati
cxciii Commemoratio mandatorum legis per moysen populo data
cxciiii Ubi ad regem iuda scriptura reuertitur et dicit ezechiam
regnasse annos xviiii
cxcv Hic ostenditur ezechiam et lucos et serpentem aeneum quem
moyses erexerat comminuisse
cxcvi Ubi salmanasar rex syriae samariam debellat tempo
ribus ezechiae regis iuda
cxcvii Ubi ezechias rex iuda esaiam consulit obsessus a rege assyriorum
cxcviii Ubi esaias propheta ezechiae uictoriam pollicetur
cxcviiii Ubi rapsaces in regionem suam reuertitur
cc Ubi esaias prophetat de rege assyriorum ad ezechiam
cci Ubi ezechiae mors ab esaia pronuntiatur
ccii Ubi adduntur ezechiae ad uitam xv anni
cciii Munera missa ezechiae a rege babilonis
cciiii Propalatio esaiae uenturum populi iuda in captiui
tatem babiloniae
ccv Hic moritur ezechias et regnat manasses filius eius
xii annorum et est rex in iuda xiiii
ccvi Ubi post inmundas sanctiones manasse regis prophe
tant multi captiuitatem iudae
ccvii Ubi moritur manasses et regnat ammon filius eius annis duobus
ccviii Ubi ammon a seruis occiditur et fit rex iosias filius
eius qui fuit xvi et regnauit annis xxxi
ccviiii Ubi iubetur rex iosias pecuniam templi colligi et far
tis tectis expendi templi
ccx Ubi ostenduntur rationes non reddi a praepositis
ccxi Hic traditur liber legis regi iosiae quo lecto omnia simula
cra et lucos incendit
ccxii Ubi non tanguntur ossa illius prophetae qui in nomine domi
mine ad hieroboam uenerat cuius mentio fit
in superiori capitulo xlviiii
ccxiii Ubi ostenditur etiam recto corde iosiae regis iuda
de hierusalem captiuitatem non amotam
ccxiiii Hic occiditur iosias et regnat ioachaz filius eius
mensibus tribus qui est xvii annorum xxiii
ccxv Remoto achaz rege regnat ioachim frater eius xviiii
ccxvi Hic ostenditur noluisse dominum propitiare populo iuda
propter manasse
ccxvii Hic moritur ioacim et accipit regnum iam cap
tiuum populo ioacin filius eius qui postea
sedechias dictus est et regnauit annis xi
ccxviii Ubi nabuchodonosor regi babyloniae traditur
populus iuda cum rege sedecia et templum
hierusalem incenditur
ccxviiii Postquam sedecias qui et ioacin ductus est
captiuus caecusque in babyloniam ductus
est proponitur in hierusalem godolias
ccxx Ubi detracto carcere ioacin qui et sedecias liberatur
et alio onus statis pascitur populusque
omnis in captiuitate remansit

EXPLICIUNT TITULI

INCIPIT TEXTUS

Et rex dauid senuerat habebatque aeta
tis plurimos annos cumque operire
tur uestibus non calefiebat. Dixerunt
ergo ei serui sui: Quaeramus domino nostro
regi adulescentulam uirginem et stet co
ram rege et foueat eum dormiatque in sinu
tuo et calefaciat dominum nostrum regem.
Quaesierunt igitur adulescentulam speci
osam in omnibus finibus israhel et inuene
runt abisag sunamitem et adduxerunt eam
ad regem. Erat autem puella pulchra nimis
dormiebatque cum rege et ministrabat ei.
Rex uero non cognouit eam. Adonias autem
filius aggith eleuabatur dicens: Ego regnabo.
Fecitque sibi currum et equites et quinqua
ginta uiros qui ante eum currerent. Nec cor
ripuit eum pater suus aliquando dicens:
Quare hoc fecisti. Erat autem et ipse pul
cher ualde secundus natus post absalon et
sermo ei cum ioab filio saruiae et cum abia
thar sacerdotem qui adiuuabant partes
adoniae. Sadoc uero sacerdos et banaias
filius ioiadae et nathan propheta et semei
et chereth et robur exercitus dauid non e
rant cum adonia. Immolatur ergo adonias
arietibus et uitulis et uniuersis pinguibus
iuxta lapidem zoheleth qui erat uicinus fon
ti rogel et uocauit uniuersos fratres suos fili
os regis et omnes uiros iuda seruos regis. Na
than autem prophetam et banaiam et ro
bustos quosque et salomonem fratrem suum
non uocauit. Dixit itaque nathan ad bethsa
bee matrem salomonis: Num audisti quod
regnauerit adonias filius aggith et domi
nus noster dauid hoc ignorat? Nunc ergo
ueni et accipe a me consilium et salua ani
mam tuam filiique tui salomonis. Uade et
ingredere ad regem dauid et dicito ei: Non
ne tu domine mi rex iurasti mihi ancillae
tuae dicens quod salomon filius tuus reg
nauit post me et ipse sedebit in throno meo.
Quare ergo regnauit adonias? Et adhuc ibi te
loquente cum rege ego ueniam post te et con
plebo sermones tuos. Ingressa est itaque beth
sabee ad regem in cubiculo. Rex autem senuerat
nimis et abisag sunamitis ministrabat ei.
Inclinauit se bethsabee et adorauit regem.
Ad quam rex: Quid tibi inquit uis? Quae respon
dens ait: Domine mi tu iurasti per dominum deum
tuum ancillae tuae dicens: Salomon filius tuus
regnabit post me et ipse sedebit in solio meo. Et
ecce nunc adonias regnauit te domine mi rex
ignorante. Mactauit boues et pinguia quaeque
et arietes plurimos et uocauit omnes filios
regis, abiathar quoque sacerdotem et ioab prin
cipem militiae. Salomonem autem seruum
tuum non uocauit. Uerumtamen domine mi
rex in te oculi respiciunt totius israhel ut
indices eis qui sedere debeat in solio tuo domine
mi rex post te. Eritque cum dormierit domi
nus meus rex cum patribus suis erimus ego et
filius meus salomon peccatores. Adhuc illa lo
quente cum rege ecce nathan propheta uenit
et nuntiauerunt regi dicentes: Adest nathan
propheta. Cumque introisset ante conspec
tum regis et adorasset eum pronus in terram
dixit nathan: Domine mi rex tu dixisti adoni
as regnet post me et ipse sedeat super thronum
meum? Quia descendit hodie et immolauit bo
ues et pinguia et arietes plurimos et uocauit
omnes filios regis et principes exercitus, abi
athar quoque sacerdotem, illisque uescentibus
et bibentibus coram eo et dicentibus: Uiuat rex
adonias, me seruum tuum et sadoch sacerdotem
et banaiam filium ioiadae et salomonem famu
lum tuum non uocauit. Numquid a domino meo
rege exiuit hoc uerbum et mihi non indicasti ser
uo tuo quis sessurus esset super thronum domi
ni mei regis post eum? Et respondit rex dauid di
cens: Uocate ad me bethsabee. Quae cum fuisset
ingressa coram rege et stetisset ante eum iu
rauit rex et ait: Uiuit dominus qui eruit animam
meam de omni angustia, quia sicut iuraui tibi
per dominum deum israhel dicens: Salomon filius tu
us regnabit post me et ipse sedebit super solium
meum pro me, sic faciam hodie. Summissoque beth
sabee in terram uultu adorauit regem dicens:
Uiuat dominus meus rex dauid in aeternum.
Dixitque quoque rex dauid: Uocate mihi sadoch sa
cerdotem et nathan prophetam et banaiam filium
ioiadae. Qui cum ingressi fuissent coram rege di
xit ad eos: Tollite uobiscum seruos domini uestri
et inponite salomonem filium meum super mu
lam meam et ducite eum in gion et unguat eum ibi
sadoch sacerdos et nathan propheta in regem super
israhel et canetis bucina atque dicetis: Uiuat
rex salomon. Et ascendetis post eum et ueniet
et sedebit super solium meum et ipse regnabit
pro me, illique praecipiam ut sit dux super israhel
et super iudam. Et respondit banaias filius ioiadae
regi dicens: Amen. Sic loquatur dominus deus domini mei
regis. Quomodo fuit dominus cum domino meo rege sic
sit cum salomone et sublimius faciat solium eius

7. An Early 'Alcuin' Bible: London, British Library, MS Harley 2805, fol. 30r. *c.* 815/20: ?Cologne.

'Alcuin' Bibles are more numerous than Theodulf Bibles (**no. 6**) and much more diverse.[1] The *only* common factor is their association with the monastery of St. Martin, Tours, of which Alcuin was abbot 796–804. There he established a tradition of book-production which was maintained and developed by his successors, from Fridugisus (807–834) to Vivian (843–851). These were independent men, with ideas of their own. Although they inherited from Alcuin the concept of the pandect, and continued themselves to commission pandects, they were not using one archetypal Alcuinian exemplar of the text. By the same token they were not relying on a single comprehensive series of illustrations (Kessler). 'Alcuin' Bibles are one aspect of book-production in a *scriptorium* that was active and changing over half a century; all that they have in common is our modern scholarly recognition that the genre as such had Alcuin's approval.

Parchment and paper; v + 237 + iii fol.; page 526 x 356 mm.; text 381 x 271 mm.; column 381 x 122 mm.; 51 lines; here shown Exod. 26:26–28:8. The ruling is minimal: single vertical boundary-lines to each column, with ample space between the columns (23 mm.). Within the broad parameters of Tours script several distinct, indeed disparate, scribes have collaborated here. Generally they change over at the end of a quire, or at the end of a book. Their text is absolutely continuous: neither deployed *per cola et commata* (**no. 3** and cf. **no. 6**) nor offset into the left margin, nor even divided into sections by a rubricator. 'Capitula' are provided only for Genesis–Judges. Decoration is limited to a few simple ink initials with Celtic interlace (e.g. Locutus: fol. 47r, Num. 1:1). A provenance in Cologne is suggested—but not proven—by the eleventh-century necrology on the opening flyleaf (fol. ivr: Rand, his fol. 1*).

Harley 2805 is the first, and only surviving, half of a pandect that was later bound as two volumes. It contains most of the Old Testament; the lost second volume presumably contained the Wisdom-literature, the apocrypha (Wisdom, Ecclesiasticus, Judith, Tobit, I–II Maccabees) and the New Testament, probably with canon-tables preceding the Gospels. By comparison with the Theodulf Bible (**no. 6**), this is a book for public use: a vast folio volume in a script large enough to be read easily in public. It is a practical, reliable text, written for a community that had only one Bible and wanted a good one.

Such a volume was never superseded. An eleventh-century librarian has done a skillful repair to the second column of the page reproduced here; an entire folio was replaced in the twelfth century (fol. 21r); a later rubricator updated the chapter-numbers; and finally in the fifteenth century twelve paper folios were supplied in a good cursive hand.[2] Harley 2805 was read more or less ceaselessly for over six hundred years.

Bibliography: J. Duft et al., *Die Bibel von Moutier-Grandval* (Bern, 1971) [= London, British Library, MS Add. 10546]; Fischer, 'Alkuin-Bibeln' and 'Bibelausgaben'; H. L. Kessler, *The Illustrated Bibles from Tours* (Princeton, 1977); W. Koehler, *Die karolingischen Miniaturen I: Die Schule von Tours,* 2 vols. and plates (Berlin, 1930–33) 1.98–120, 372 [= no. 13]; pl. I 13a; E. K. Rand, *Studies in the Script of Tours, I: A Survey of the Manuscripts,* 2 vols. (Cambridge, Mass., 1929) 1.118–19 [= no. 49], 2.LX.

[1] Fischer reckons 23 'Alcuin' Bibles, not counting another 15 gospelbooks ('Bibelausgaben', p. 94).

[2] The paper folios supplied in the fifteenth century are fol. 1–3, 6, 8, 36, 114, 118, 233, 235–37.

tabernaculi. Et quinque alios in altero et eius
dem numeri ad occidentalem plagam qui mitten
tur per medias tabulas. A summo usque ad sum
mum. ipsasque tabulas deaurabis et fundes in eis
anulos aureos. per quos uectes tabulata contine
ant. quos operies lamminis aureis. Et eriges
tabernaculum iuxta exemplum quod tibi in monte
monstratum est. Facies et uelum de hyacintho
et purpura cocco que bis tincto et bis so retor to
opere plumario. et pulchra uarietate contextum.
quod appendens ante quattuor columnas de lignis
setthim. quae ipsae quidem deauratae erunt
et habebunt capita aurea sed bases argenteas.
Inseretur autem uelum per circulos intra quod
pones arcam testimonii. et quo sanctuarium. et sancta
rii sanctuaria diuidentur. Pones et propitiato
rium super arcam testimonii in sancta sanctorum.
mensamque extra uelum et contra mensam
candelabrum. in latere tabernaculi meridiano.
mensa enim stabit in parte aquilonis.
Facies et tentorium in introitu tabernaculi
de hyacinto et purpura cocco que bis tincto
et byssoretorta opere plumarii. et quinque
columnas deaurabis lignorum setthim.
Ante quas ducetur tentorium quarum erunt
capita aurea et bases aeneae. [cap. 27] Facies et alta
re de lignis setthim. quod habebit quinque
cubitos in longitudine et totidem in latitu
dine id est quadrum. et tres cubitos in altitu
dine. Cornua autem per quattuor angulos
ex ipso erunt et operies illud aere.
CVI. Faciesque in usus eius lebetes ad suscipien
dos cineres. et forcipes atque fuscinulas
et ignium receptacula. omnia uasa ex aere
CVII. fabricabis. Craticulamque in modum retis
aeneam. per cuius quattuor angulos erunt
quattuor anuli aenei. quos pones super
arulam altaris eritque craticula usque
CVIII. ad altaris medium. Facies et uectes
altaris de lignis setthim duos quos operies
lamminis aeneis. Et induces per circulos
eruntque ex utroque latere altaris ad por
tandum. Non solidum sed inane et cauum
intrinsecus facies illud sicut tibi in monte
monstratum est. Facies et atrium taberna
culi. In cuius plaga australi contra meridiem
erunt tentoria de bysso retorta. Centum
cubitos unum latus tenebit in longitudine.
Et columnas. xx. cum basibus totidem
aeneis. quae capita cum caelaturis suis
habebunt argentea. Similiter in latere

aquilonis per longum. erunt tentoria centum
cubitorum columnae xx. et bases aeneae
eiusdem numeri et capita earum cum caela
turis suis argentea. In latitudine uero atrii
quo respicit ad occidentem erunt tentoria
per quinquaginta cubitos. Et columnae decem
basesque totidem. In ea quoque atrii lati
tudine quae respicit ad orientem. quinqua
ginta cubiti erunt. In quibus quindecim cubito
rum tentoria lateri uno deputabuntur.
Columnaeque tres et bases totidem. Et in la
tere altero erunt tentoria cubitos optinen
tia. xv. Columnas tres. et bases totidem.
In introitu uero atrii fiet tentorium cubitorum
xx. ex hyacinto et purpura. cocco que bis tincto
et bysso retorta opere plumarii. Columnas
habebit quattuor cum basibus totidem. Omnes
columnae atrii per circuitum uestitae erunt argenti
lamminis capitibus argenteis et basibus aeneis.
In longitudine occupabit atrium cubitos centum.
In latitudine. L. Altitudo. v. cubitorum erit.
fietque de bysso retorta. et habebit bases aeneas.
Cuncta uasa tabernaculi in omnes usus et caeri
monias. tam paxillos eius quam atrii ex aere facies.
CVI. Praecipe filiis israhel ut adferant tibi oleum
de arboribus oliuarum purissimum piloque
contusum ut ardeat lucerna semper in tabernaculo
testimonii extra uelum quod oppansum est
testimonio. Et collocabunt eam aaron et filii eius
ut usque mane luceat coram domino. Perpetuus
erit cultus per successiones eorum a filiis israhel.
CVII. Adplica quoque ad te aaron fratrem tuum Cap xxviii .xxviii.
cum filiis suis de medio filiorum israhel. ut sacerdo
tio fungantur mihi. aaron. nadab. et abiu. et ele
CVIII. azar. et thamar. Faciesque uestem sanctam fratri tuo in
gloriam et decorem. et loqueris cunctis sapientibus corde
quos repleui spiritu prudentiae. ut faciant uestes aaron in qui
CVIIII. bus sanctificatus ministret mihi. Haec autem erunt
uestimenta quae facient. rationale et super hu
merale. tunicam et lineam strictam. cidarim
et balteum facient uestimenta sancta aaron fra
tri tuo et filiis eius. Ut sacerdotio fungantur mihi.
Accipientque aurum et hyacintum et purpu
ram coccumque bis tinctum et byssum. facient
autem superhumerale de auro et hyacinto
ac purpura cocco que bis tincto et bysso retorto
opere polymito. Duas oras iunctas habebit
in utroque latere summitatum et in unum redе
ant. ipsaque textura et cuncta operis uarietas.
erit ex auro et hyacinto ac purpura coccoque

8. Rabanus Maurus, Commentary on Deuteronomy and Joshua: London, British Library, MS Add. 38687, fol. 120v. s. xii4/4: Pontigny (dioc. Auxerre).

Rabanus analyzed the entire Old Testament (except for Baruch) and much of the New. He is seen today as tediously derivative—all his doctrine is patristic. But what the Carolingian reader wanted was precisely the Fathers made intelligible, that is, abridged, clarified and updated. Rabanus deleted for example many of Jerome's linguistic observations—learned but no longer comprehensible—and explained obsolete words and the practices of a late antique urban culture which was known indirectly and imperfectly to the reader in Saxony or the Rhineland. To have a virtually complete commentary on the Old Testament was in itself a new development, one that was not equaled until the twelfth-century *Glossa ordinaria.* Even then, some librarians valued Rabanus.

Parchment; page 328 x 240 mm.; text 223 x 155 mm.; column 223 x 70 mm.; 36 lines. Ruled in pencil, with broad (28 mm.) double boundary-column on the outer edge of the text, in which quotation marks are hung. A few well-executed major initials (5/8 lines high), marking the beginning of Rabanus's preface (fol. 1ra) and of the books of his commentary (fol. 3rb, 21rb, 48va, 71ra). Simpler, two-color initials at the beginning of Joshua (fol. 96ra, 98ra), and one 4-line initial (fol. 116rb).

The page shown contains the commentary on Joshua 10:11–15 (Rabanus 2.3; *PL* 108:1044D–45B). A thirteenth-century hand has added the new capitulation (cf. **no. 18**) in the upper margin. The marginalia to the left and right identify Rabanus's own contribution, 'Maurus', and one of his sources, Origen, here called 'Adamantius' (Homily on Joshua xi.3–4). The epithet was recorded by Eusebius, and so passed to the Latin west in Rufinus's translation of the *Ecclesiastical History.*[1]

According to a contemporary colophon (fol. 150rb) the manuscript belonged to the Cistercian abbey of Pontigny. Six other Pontigny manuscripts of Rabanus in the same series can still be identified:[2] **Exodus**—Armagh, Public Library, MS G.II.7 (*ex* Allard, bought 1869 by Dean Reeves of Armagh); **Leviticus**—sold 1869, present location unknown; **Numbers**—Eugene, Ore., University of Oregon Library, MS 3 (*ex* Allard, *ex* Phillipps 3724); **Deuteronomy, Joshua**—London, British Library, MS Add. 38687 (*ex* Allard, *ex* Phillipps 3725); **Jeremiah, Lamentations** *either*—Cambridge, Mass., Harvard University, Houghton Library, fMS Typ 200 (*ex* Allard, *ex* Phillipps 3726, *ex* Philip Hofer) *or*—Armagh, Public Library, MS G.II.26 (*ex* Allard, as Exodus); **Matthew**—London, University of London, University College, MS lat. 7 (*ex* Allard, *ex* Phillipps 3727); **Acts**—Armagh, Public Library, MS G.II.27 (*ex* Allard, as Exodus).

Only a Rabanus exhibition could reunite these manuscripts today.

Bibliography: G. Colvener, *Hrabani Mauri Opera* (Cologne, 1627) 2.405–463 = Deuteronomy only; Joshua could not be found (vol. I, prolegomena); *PL* 108:839–1108. R. Kottje, 'Hrabanus', *Verfasserlexikon* (1983), 4.166–96; L. Light, *The Bible in the Twelfth Century: An Exhibition of Manuscripts at the Houghton Library* [Harvard] (Cambridge, Mass., 1988), no. 25, with plate; A. N. L. Munby, *The Formation of the Phillipps Library up to the Year 1840* (Phillipps Studies, 3; Cambridge, 1954); *The Phillipps Manuscripts: Catalogus librorum manuscriptorum in bibliotheca D. Thomae Phillipp, Phillipps, Bart., impressus typis Medio-Montanis 1837-1871* (1837– ; rpt. London, 1968); M. Peyrafort-Bonnet, 'La dispersion d'une bibliothèque médiévale: les manuscrits de l'abbaye de Pontigny', *Cîteaux commentarii cistercienses* 35 (1984) 92–128; C. H. Talbot, 'Notes on the Library of Pontigny', *Analecta sacri ordinis cisterciensis* 10 (1954) 106–68, at 162–63 *et passim.*

[1] Eusebius, *Historia ecclesiastica* 6.14.10; *PG* 20:552–54.

[2] All seven manuscripts remained in the Pontigny library until its secularization in 1790, when they seem to have trickled into the hands of local antiquarians. The abbé Joseph-Felix Allard (1795–1831) sold four of them to Sir Thomas Phillipps of Cheltenham, on the slow dispersal of whose collection they were scattered across the world.

et hanc eorum fidem non eos perdendo
remuneravit quodammodo,
Cumque fugerent filios israel et essent
in descensu bethoron: dominus misit
super eos lapides magnos de celo usque
azecha. Et mortui sunt multo plures
lapidibus grandinis: quam quos gladio
aḡ. percusserant filii israel. Lapides sunt gran
dinis dure vindicte que celitus mit
tuntur super hostes populi dei. vel divi
ne comminationes que in scripturas sa
cris contra impios leguntur prolate. vel
gehenna ignis et pena eis predicitur
adā. perpetua. Hoc ergo modo ihesus cum duci
bus et virtutibus suis adest his qui
pro nomine suo a contrariis virtutibus
obpugnantur: et non solum auxilium
prestat in bello? verum et producit
tempus diei. et spacia lucis protelans
adventum discutit noctis. unde sequitur. Tunc
locutus est iosue domino in die qua tradidit
amorreum in conspectu filiorum israel. di
xitque coram eis. Sol contra gabaon
ne movearis. et luna contra vallem ahi
alon. Steteruntque sol et luna. Non
ne scriptum est hoc in libro iustorum?
Stetit itaque sol in medio celi: et non
festinavit occumbere spacio unius
diei. Non fuit ante et postea tam longa
dies: obediente domino voci hominis. et
pugnante pro israel. Reversusque est iosue cum
adā. omni israel in castra galgale. Volumus
ergo si possumus ostendere. quomodo dominus noster
ihesus protelaverit lucem. et maiorem fecerit
diem: vel pro salute hominum. vel pro
interitu contrariarum virtutum. Ex quo

advenit salvator filius erat mundi.
iam denique ipse dicebat. Penitentiam
agite. appropinquavit enim regnum celorum. Et tenuit et
repressit diem consummationis. et adesse
prohibuit. videns enim deus pater salutem
gentium. per ipsum solum posse constare.
dicit ad eum. Pete a me et dabo tibi gentes
hereditatem tuam. et possessionem tuam terminos terre. Donec
ergo prima pollicitatio compleatur. ec
clesie ex diversis nationibus crescat atque
introeat tota gentium multitudo:
tunc demum omnis israel salvetur. dies
producitur et differtur occasus. Non enim umquam
sol occubuit: sed semper oritur. dum cre
dentium cordibus sol iusticie lumen ve
ritatis infundit. Cum vero repleta fuerit
mensura credentium. et deterior iam ac
decolor etas ultime generationis adve
nerit? cum increscente iniquitate refriges
cet caritas multorum. et perpauci rema
serint in quibus fides inveniatur: tunc
iam breviabuntur dies. Idem ergo atque ip
se dominus novit et extendere diem cum salu
tis est tempus. et breviare diem: et produci
tur nobis spacium lucis sic ut in die
honeste ambulemus: et opera lucis ope
remur. Sed et illud videamus: quid
sit quinque reges fuisse? et hos in spe
lunca eorum fugisse. Sepe diximus duplicem
esse christianorum pugnam. Perfectis qui
dem et talibus qualis erat paulus a
postolus qui dicit. non erat eis pugna adver
sus carnem et sanguinem. sed adversus
principes et potestates adversus mundi huius rectores tenebra
rum harum: et spiritalia nequitie in celestibus.
Inferioribus vero et nondum perfectis pugna

C. VERNACULAR BIBLES

9. Otfrid of Weissenburg, *Evangelienbuch:* Munich, Bayerische Staatsbibliothek, MS Cgm 14, fol. 16v.
902/906: Freising Cathedral.

The latter part of Jesus's childhood as narrated in the Gospel harmony of Otfrid of Weissenburg. The Latin heading DE MORTE HERODIS introduces 16 lines of German verse, set out in long lines with a break, or *caesura,* in the middle. The first line is again in capitals, THOR STARP THER KUNING HEROD. IOH HINA ÝVARTÁ INAN TÓD: 'Then this King Herod died, and Death led him away' (1.21). Years later, the Holy Family returns to Galilee, whence they visit Jerusalem. There (1.22) the twelve-year-old Jesus teaches in the Temple (Luke 2:42–50): XXII. CVM FACTVS ESSET JESVS ANNORVM XII. ET RELIQVA. The reader is further assisted by the running Latin summary in the margin: 'After Herod's death' . . . 'They departed into Galilee'.

Parchment; page 320 x 222 mm.; text 235 x 150 mm.; 29 lines, ruled with a column to accommodate offset letters, and a further wider panel to contain the Latin summaries and biblical *lemmata,* here the four notes beginning 'Defuncto autem Herode'. The text is composed in long lines, with internal rhyme, but deployed as though it were Latin elegiacs, in that every other line begins with an offset majuscule. At this early date the *mise-en-page* of Old High German verse is wholly unpredictable.

According to the colophon (fol. 125r: Petzet and Glauning, pl. VIII) this manuscript was written by the priest Sigihart for Waldo, bishop of Freising (883–906), then the dominant religious and cultural center in southern Bavaria. The date of 902/906 depends on the argument that the exemplar, Vienna, Österreichische Nationalbibliothek, MS 2687, became available to Hatto, archbishop of Mainz in 902, on his becoming abbot of Weissenburg, and thus in turn to Waldo in the last years of his own episcopate.[1] Beatus Rhenanus cites our manuscript—which he had seen in the library of Freising—as proof that the *Franci* of old had spoken German.[2]

Sigihart used the same script for Latin and German, except that Old High German makes more use of z, both 'small' (line 2, Thaz) and tailed (line 2, zit). In his *mise-en-page* the Latin frames the vernacular, presenting and authenticating it to the reader. At the same time he is making visual reference to Latin verse, with its marked *caesura.* The internal rhyme (e.g. iungo/sólango, line 1) is marked with a long space; other manuscripts of the *Evangelienbuch* have a raised point (*punctus*) hovering above the line. The stress-marks (cf. **no. 12**), indicate that the German text was recited aloud or sung to its monastic and perhaps also its courtly audience.

Bibliography: Otfrid von Weissenburg, *Evangelienbuch,* ed. O. Erdmann, 6th ed., corr. L. Wolff (Altdeutsche Textbibliothek, 49; Tübingen, 1973); Otfrid von Weissenburg, *Evangelienbuch,* ed. G. Vollmann-Profe, Reclam (Stuttgart, 1987) [selected chapters with facing German translation, good commentary, inexpensive]; H. Butzmann, *Otfrid von Weissenburg, Evangelienharmonie: vollständige Faksimile-Ausgabe des Codex Vindobonensis 2687 der österreichischen Nationalbibliothek* (Codices selecti, 30; Graz, 1972); E. Petzet and O. Glauning, *Deutsche Schrifttafeln des IX. bis XVI. Jahrhunderts aus Handschriften der K. Hof- und Staatsbibliothek in München,* 5 Teile in 1 Band (Munich, 1910–12, Leipzig, 1924–30; rpt. Hildesheim, 1975) 1, pl. VIII. B. Bischoff, *Die südostdeutschen Schreibschulen und Bibliotheken in der Karolingerzeit, I,* 3rd ed. (Wiesbaden, 1974), pp. 129–30; K. Bertau, 'Epenrezitaten im deutschen Mittelalter', *Études germaniques* 20 (1965) 1–17; J. K. Bostock, *A Handbook on Old High German Literature,* 2nd ed., revised by K. C. King and D. R. McLintock (Oxford, 1976), pp. 190–212; N. Daniel, *Handschriften des zehnten Jahrhunderts aus der Freisinger Dombibliothek* (Munich, 1973), pp. 63–65; J. Heinzle, W. Haubrichs, G. Vollmann-Profe, *Geschichte der deutschen Literatur von den Anfängen bis zum Beginn der Neuzeit* (Frankfurt, 1984); E. Hellgardt, *Die exegetischen Quellen von Otfrids Evangelienbuch* (Tübingen, 1981); W. Kleiber, *Otfrid von Weissenburg* (Bern/Munich, 1971); W. Schröder, 'Otfrid von Weissenburg', *Verfasserlexikon* (1987) 7.172–93; S. Sonderegger, *Althochdeutsche Sprache und Literatur* (Sammlung Göschen, 8005; Berlin/New York, 1974).

---

[1]*Sed contra.* The Vienna manuscript was written 863/71 and apparently kept in Weissenburg. Bishop Waldo was free to order a copy by 883, or indeed sooner.

[2]Beatus Rhenanus, *Rerum germanicarum libri tres* (Basel, 1531), pp. 106–108.

Ther iro kúning iungo · Ni midit ió so lango
Thaz uuig er ni fárbari · Inthiu sin zit uuari
Ergi schein thaz filu stam · So er zi sinen tagon quam
Tho gozer bluinsih sinaz bluat · Thaz kuning ander niriuat
Nu folget imo thúruh thaz · Gidigini sómanagaz
Thaz thér nist hiar in libe · Der dia zala ir scribe

XXI DE MORTE HERODIS

Defuncto aũ herode · THOR STARP THER KUNING HEROD · IOH HINA FUARTA INAN TÓD
Mittodu er daga fulta · Ther ió inabuh vuólta
Thar ioséph uuas in lante · Hina in élilente
Quam imbot imo introume · Er thes kindes uuola goume
Thia muater ouh bibringe · Ziro heiminge
Ioh uuison heimortes · Eiganes lantes
Nist thires quader not · Ther iro stant ther ist dot
Bithiu ili ió thes sindes · Thes iro heiminges

Qui consurgens accepit puerum · Fuar er sár heimort · Firnam ouh kerno thiu uuort
Samant mit ther muater · So fuar ther sun guater
Audiens autem quod archelaus regnaret · Thogi hórter mári · Thar ander kuning uuári
Ioh óuh thero uuorto · Hintar quám er harto
Kherter tho in stara · In eina burg ziara
Thaz kind er scono thar iz zoh · Ioh thén fiantón int floh
Secessit in partes galilaee · Uuuah ser filu zioro · In uuizzen uuola schiaro
In uuistuam thih ió thanne · Mit góte ioh mit manne

XXII CUM FACTUS ESSET IHC ANNORŨ XII ET RELIQUA

SO ER THO UUARD ALTERO · Zuuiror seh siaro
Sie flizzun thaz sie giltin · Zen hóhen gizitin
Thie ziti sint so héilag · Thaz man irzellen nimach
Uuir forahtlicho iz uuiezen · Ioh ostóron heizen
Zen uuihen zitin fuarun · So siu giuuon uuárun

10. The Anglo-Saxon Hexateuch (Genesis–Joshua): London, British Library, MS Cotton Claudius B.IV, fol. 138v. s. xi2/4: St. Augustine's, Canterbury.

The Old English translation of Genesis–Joshua, which is in broad terms attributable to Aelfric, abbot of Eynsham (*ob. c.* 1010).[1] Almost every page of the manuscript has a picture, sometimes two. These show the creation, the Fall, the migrations to and from Egypt, the definition of law and ritual and the establishment of the Jews in the land west of the river Jordan.

Parchment; 156 fol.; page 328 x 217 mm.; text *c.* 267 x 167 mm.; 36 lines. Identified by the 2° *folio* as being in St. Augustine's, Canterbury in the later fifteenth century (Ker). Moses is shown making his final dispositions before his death (Deut. 31:9). He writes down the law, and gives it to the Levites to keep with the Ark of the Covenant. Two young men carry the Ark shoulder-high on poles, while the leaders of the tribes stand in attendance. Moses himself is seated in the posture of an evangelist writing. His two great horns refer to Jerome's rabbinic interpretation of the splendor emanating from Moses's face when he had talked with God on Mount Sinai (p. 2 n.8 above). This is the earliest manuscript to show Moses with horns (Mellinkoff). Sometimes they have been added later, but here they are original. The text has run ahead of the illumination into the Canticle of Moses (Deut 32: here 32:34–47; Crawford, pp. 372–74).

The mere number of color pictures (394 in all) makes this a remarkable volume, such as later generations who had ceased to read Anglo-Saxon treasured as an heirloom. But it is not a luxury manuscript in the manner of (say) the Benedictional of St. Aethelwold.[2] Script and parchment are of only moderate quality,[3] and there is some evidence that the illustrations were built up using templates—e.g. Israelites approaching Moses (fol. 107v) and much of the Book of Joshua (fol. 142r–55v; see Facsimile, pp. 53–64, with references). Such economies point to a *scriptorium* or workshop that was ready to produce as many illustrated Hexateuchs as might be required. For whom? As a diplomatic gift or for the prosperous layman? The ealdorman Aethelweard, to whom Aelfric addressed a prologue to the English Hexateuch (Facsimile, p. 44; Crawford, pp. 76–80), may have represented a tradition of lay literacy that was to grow in significance in the eleventh century. Far too little data survives for this question to be resolved.

Bibliography: Facsimile edited by C. R. Dodwell and P. Clemoes, *The Old English Illustrated Hexateuch* (EEMF, 18; Copenhagen, 1974); S. J. Crawford, *The Old English Version of the Heptateuch, Aelfric's Treatise on the Old and New Testament and His Preface to Genesis* (Early English Text Society, O.S., 160; London, 1922; expanded rpt., 1969). N. R. Ker, *Catalogue of Manuscripts Containing Anglo-Saxon* (Oxford, 1957), no. 142; R. Mellinkoff, *The Horned Moses in Medieval Art and Thought* (Berkeley, 1970); E. Temple, *Anglo-Saxon Manuscripts, 900–1066* (A Survey of Manuscripts Illuminated in the British Isles, 2; London, 1976), no. 86.

[1]It is thought that Aelfric was directly responsible for part of Genesis, and for Numbers and Joshua. The balance was revised by an anonymous scholar—arguably Byrhtferth of Ramsey—who knew Aelfric's work.

[2]F. Wormald, *The Benedictional of St. Ethelwold* (London, 1959).

[3]Contrast Oxford, Bodleian Library, MS Laud. Misc. 509, an eleventh-century text of the English Hexateuch without illustrations, but far superior in script and *mise-en-page.*

on minum goldhordum. Seo wracu is min, ⁊ ic hit agylde on ðam
dæg hyra fot æt slide. Hyra forwyrde dæg is gehende. ⁊ þas
ðinge eow synd gegearwode. drihten demð his folce. ⁊ gemilt
sað his ðeowum. he gesyhð hi geunstrangod. ⁊ ða belocenan
geteorodun ⁊ ða lafa synd fornumene. ⁊ he cweðað hwær synd
hyra godas on ðam hi truwan hæfdon. of ðæra offrunga
ge æton fyrslas. ⁊ druncon win on heora offrungum. Arison
⁊ fylston eow æt nyd ðearfe. gesceoð ðæt ic ana com ⁊ nis nan oþer
god butan me. Ic ofslea ⁊ ic lætte libban. Ic ofslea ⁊ ic hæle, ⁊ ne
mæg nan man of minre handa ætalysan. Ic hæbbe to heo
fone mine hand, ⁊ ic swerige ðurh mine swyðran ⁊ ic cweðe
ic libbe on ecnysse. Ic gescyrpe min swurd swa ligette ⁊ min
hand demð. Ic agylde wrace minum feondum ⁊ ðam ðe me
hatedon. Ic gemyrige mine flan on blode ⁊ min swurd swyt
flæsc. Geblissiað heofonas mid him ⁊ arwurðion hine ealle
godes englas. Ðeoda heriað his folc forðam ðe he wrycð his
ðeowas. ⁊ agylt wrace hyra feondū ⁊ drihten byð arfæst his
folces lande. Moyses ⁊ iosue nunes sunu nu spræcon
ealle ðas word to eallum israhela folce, ⁊ cwædon, healdaþ ealle
ðas word ðe ic eow to dæg bebeode ⁊ beodað ða eowrum bearnum
to healdenne ⁊ to donne. forðam ne synd hi eow on idel beboden
ac ðæt ge libbon ðurh hine ⁊ ðurh hi wunion lange tid. ⁊ do ða
þinge on ðam lande ðe ge infaraþ to agenne þonne ge ofer iordanen
farað.

11. An English-Latin Psalter: Paris, Bibliothèque Nationale, MS lat. 8824, fol. 1v–2r. s. xi2/4: perhaps Canterbury.

A bilingual Psalter in Latin and Anglo-Saxon, with Anglo-Saxon 'introductions' to Psalms 2–50, here Psalms 2:1–3:4.

Parchment; iii + 186 + ii fol.; page 526 x 186 mm.; text 420 x 95 mm.; 45 lines. A single boundary-column (2 lines) to the left and right of the text, a double boundary-column (3 lines) down the center of the page. An exceptionally tall, narrow book. The presence of St. Martial in the litany (fol. 184r) gives a date of 1029+.

The Latin text is the Romanum, displaced in England by the Gallicanum only after the Norman Conquest. The Anglo-Saxon is more curious. Psalms 1–50 and their 'introductions' (none to Psalm 1) have been persistently associated with the court of King Alfred, but without any clear evidence. The 'introductions' (unique to this manuscript) derive from the Latin version of Theodore of Mopsuestia's commentary on the Psalms—a rare text, but available in Canterbury in the later eleventh century.[1] Psalms 51–150 are in Anglo-Saxon verse. A fragment (Psalms 90:15–95:2) of this metrical section is repeated in the Eadwine Psalter, a luxury volume written and illuminated in Christ Church, Canterbury *c.* 1160.[2] The little drawings within the text (Psalm 2:4 and 9), two of thirteen in the opening pages (fol. 1–6), are literal illustrations of the Psalter text, some (e.g. Psalm 2:9) reflecting the illustrations of the same text in the Utrecht Psalter, and all in the same stylistic tradition.[3] Finally our manuscript once had nine full illuminations: David the harpist at the beginning, and the others at the six liturgical divisions of the Psalter, at Psalm 51, and between the Psalter and the Canticles.[4] This manuscript was originally more of a luxury volume than it now appears.

Prima facie it is a Canterbury book. The Utrecht Psalter was in Christ Church by *c.* 1000; the Eadwine Psalter is the only other witness (albeit brief) to the metrical translation. But scholars have hesitated to go along this road, protesting that the dialect is that of Wessex rather than Kent. Yet by the mid-eleventh century all literary Anglo-Saxon, old and new, was being standardized to the Wessex tradition, as the written language of the court.

By the early fifteenth century this elegant if incomprehensible Psalter had reached the library of the Duc de Berry, who presented it to the Sainte Chapelle in Bourges. Martène saw it there three hundred years later, and it passed to the royal collection in 1752.[5]

Bibliography: Facsimile ed. B. Colgrave, *The Paris Psalter: MS. Bibliothèque Nationale fonds latin 8824* (EEMF, 8; Copenhagen, 1958). N. R. Ker, *Catalogue of Manuscripts Containing Anglo-Saxon* (Oxford, 1957), no. 367, pp. 440–41; M. Lapidge, *Anglo-Saxon Litanies of the Saints* (Henry Bradshaw Society 106; London, 1991), p. 80; F. C. Robinson and E. G. Stanley, *Old English Verse Texts from Many Sources* (EEMF, 23; Copenhagen, 1991), p. 26, with bibliography; Temple, no. 83 and pll. 208–209.

[1] R. L. Ramsay, 'Theodore of Mopsuestia and St. Columban on the Psalms', *Zeitschrift für Celtische Philologie* 8 (1912) 421–51, with bibliography. See now the essential critique by B. Fischer, 'Bedae de titulis psalmorum liber' in *Festschrift Bernhard Bischoff zu seinem 65. Geburtstag,* ed. J. Autenrieth and F. Brunhölzl (Stuttgart, 1971), pp. 90–110. For a fragment of the Latin version of Theodore's Psalter-commentary surviving as a pastedown in a Canterbury manuscript see M. T. Gibson, 'Theodore of Mopsuestia: A Fragment in the Bodleian Library', *Journal of Theological Studies,* NS 21 (1970) 104–105.

[2] Reproduced in color by F. C. Robinson and E. G. Stanley, *Old English Verse Texts from Many Sources* (EEMF, 23; Copenhagen, 1991), p. 26 and pll. 30.1–14.

[3] *Utrecht-Psalter,* ed. K. van der Horst and J. H. A. Engelbregt (Codices selecti, 75; Graz, 1984), fol. 3v. and 2r. The Canterbury version of the Utrecht Psalter, London, British Library, MS Harley 603, is approximately coeval with MS lat. 8824.

[4] Facsimile, pp. 14–15: David the Musician *ad in.;* stubs preceding Psalms 26, 38, 51, 68, 80, 97, 109 and preceding the Canticles. The Canticles and creed (fol. 176r–183v.) are the series found in *Utrecht* and standard throughout the ninth to eleventh centuries.

[5] L. Delisle, *Le cabinet des manuscrits de la Bibliothèque nationale* (Paris, 1881) 3.172–73.

dauid wyt on englisc dauides sealm. For þæm he ys sealm gecweden forþi he seofode on þæm sealme ⁊ mænde to drihtne be his feondum ægðer ge inlendum ge utlendum ⁊ be eallum his earfoðum ⁊ swa deð ælc þara þe þysne sealm singð be his sylfes feondum ⁊ swa dyde crist be iudeum. VOX XPI DE PASSIONE AD LUCAM EVGL

QUARE FREMUERUN GENTES ET POPULI MEDITATI SUNT INANIA.

Hwy wyð ælc folc ⁊ hwi smeagað hi unnytt.

Adstiterunt reges terre et principes convenerunt in unum adversus dominum et adversus xpm eius.

Ano hwy arisað eorð cyningas ⁊ ealdormenn cumað to somne wið gode ⁊ wið þa þe he to hlaforde geceas ⁊ gesmyrede hi cweðað.

Disrumpamus vincula eorum et proiciamus a nobis iugum ipsorum.

Uton tobrecan heora bendas ⁊ aweorpan heora geocu of us.

Qui habitat in celis inridebit eos et dominus subsannabit eos.

Hwæt forsceawað heora spræce cwæð se witega þeah hi swa cweðen forþam se god þe on heofonum ys hi gehyspð ⁊ drihten hy ʒ ge sceent.

Tunc loquetur ad eos in ira sua et in furore suo conturbavit eos.

Ano he clypað to him on his yrre ⁊ gedrefð heora geþeaht.

Ego autem constitutus sum rex ab eo super sion montem sanctum eius predicans preceptum domini.

Ano ic eam þeah cinge geset fram gode ofer his ðone halgan munt syon to þam þæt ic lære his willan ⁊ his æ.

Dominus dixit ad me filius meus es tu ego hodie genui te.

Forþan cwæð drihten to me þu eart min sunu nu todæg ic ðe acende.

Postula a me et dabo tibi gentes hereditatem tuam et possessionem tuam terminos terre.

Bide me ⁊ ic þe sylle þeoda to agnum yrfe ⁊ þinne anwald ic gebræde ofer eorð to ðage mæro.

Reges eos in virga ferrea et tamquam vas figuli confringes eos.

Ano ic gedo þæt þu hi ofer ealle wylt mid isernre gyrde ⁊ hi miht swa eaðe abrecan swa se crocc wyrhta mæg ænne croccan.

Et nunc reges intellegite erudimini omnes qui iudicatis terram.

Ongytað nu kyningas ⁊ leorniað ge domeras þe eorðan demað.

Servite domino in timore et exultate ei cum tremore.

Þeowiað drihtne ⁊ ondrædað hine ⁊ blissiað on gode ⁊ ðeah mid ege.

Adprehendite disciplinam nequando irascatur dominus et pereatis de via iusta.

Onfoð lare þy læs eow god yrre weorðe ⁊ þy læs ge forweorðon of rihtum wege.

Cum exarserit in brevi ira eius beati omnes qui confidunt in eum.

Forþæm þonne his yrre byð onæled þonne beoð eadige þa þe nu on hine getrywað.

Þysne þriddan sealm dauid sang þa he fleah absalon his sunu ⁊ seofode þa yrmðe to drihtne. swa deþ ælc þara manna þe þisne sealm singð his sylfes earfoðu ægðer ge modes ge lichaman he seofað to drihtne swa dyde crist þonne he þysne sealm sang be iudeum he hine sang ⁊ be iudan scarioth þe hine læwde he seofode to drihtne.

VOX XPI AD PATREM DE IUDEIS

DOMINE QUID multiplicati sunt qui tribulant me multi insurgunt adversum me multi dicunt anime mee non est salus illi in deo eius.

Eala drihten hwi synt swa manige minra feonda þa þe me swencað forhwi arisað swa mænige wið me monige cweðað to minum mode þæt hit næbbe nane hælo æt his gode.

Tu autem domine susceptor meus es gloria mea et exal

ehte nis na swa hy cweðað ac þu eart butan ælcum tweon

12. Song of Songs with Latin and German Commentary by Williram of Ebersberg: Munich, Bayerische Staatsbibliothek, MS Cgm 10, fol. 10r. s. xi[2]: Ebersberg (dioc. Freising).

Williram of Ebersberg was head of the cathedral school in Bamberg *c.* 1050–60, then abbot of Ebersberg until his death in 1085. Such an abrupt transfer from a promising secular career to the strict monastic life —Ebersberg adhered to the Gorze reform—was a recurring pattern among the intelligentsia of the mid-eleventh century. Lanfranc entered Bec (*c.* 1042); Anselm followed him in 1063; Bruno gave up a canonry at Rheims to be a hermit and founder of La Grande Chartreuse; Manegold of Lautenbach, 'master of our masters of today', abandoned his teaching career to be prior of an Augustinian house in which he thereafter taught only the Bible. In the same way Williram found himself teaching not Virgil (for which good text-books were at hand) but the Song of Songs.

Parchment; page 331 x 252 mm.; text 248 x 190 mm.; 17 lines. Ruled at half-spacing for the outer columns of commentary, against the central column of text; double boundary-columns separating text from commentary and on the outside of both columns of commentary.

Cgm 10 was written in Ebersberg during Williram's abbacy, probably in the early 1060s (Petzet and Glauning). Although it is not thought to be the author's copy (Petzet and Glauning, citing Seemüller), the *mise-en-page* is as close as we are likely to come to Williram's original. The narrow central column is the Bible text, the first word in each sentence, or part-sentence, being in capitals: OSCVLETVR, QVIA, OLEVM, IDEO. To the left is a Latin commentary in Leonine hexameters, that is, having an internal rhyme:

> Ubera nempe tu*i* praecellunt pocula vin*i*.'
> Suauiter unguent*is* fraglantia sat precio*sis* (lines 9–12).

To the right is a German prose commentary in which each section begins with a direct translation of the Bible text.

> Wánta bȇzzer sínt dȋne spúnne démo uvíne.' sie stínchente. mít den bézzesten sálbon.[1]

Then Williram clarifies the meaning in German laced with Latin, which may well reflect how he thought and taught.

> Dív sǔoze dȋnero *gratie.* íst bezzera. dánne dív scárse déro *legis.* áls íz quit. *Lex per Moysen data est.' gratia et veritas per Iesum Christum facta est.* Dív sélbe gnȃde. ist gemíschet mít *variis donis spiritus sancti.'* mít den du máchst *ex peccatoribus iustos.*

The Latin syntax remains sound. Thus the double commentary is an exercise in metrics, an exact German translation and a bilingual analysis of the meaning. It had a steady public into the late twelfth century and beyond (Bartelmez).

Bibliography: E. H. Bartelmez, *The 'Expositio in Cantica canticorum' of Williram, Abbot of Ebersberg 1048–85* (Memoirs of the American Philosophical Society, 69; Philadelphia, 1967); E. Petzet and O. Glauning, *Deutsche Schrifttafeln des IX. bis XVI. Jahrhundert aus Handschriften der K. Hof- und Staatsbibliothek in München,* 5 Teile in 1 Band (Munich, 1910–12; Leipzig, 1924–30; rpt. Hildesheim, 1975), 1, pl. XV. K. Gärtner, 'Zu den Handschriften mit dem deutschen Kommentarteil des Hoheliedkommentars Willirams von Ebersberg' in *Deutsche Handschriften 1100–1400: Oxforder Kolloquium 1985,* ed. V. Honemann and N. F. Palmer (Tübingen, 1988), pp. 1–34; S. Sonderegger, *Althochdeutsche Sprache und Literatur* (Sammlung Göschen, 8005; Berlin/New York, 1974).

[1]The acute accent and the 'circumflex' had been in use in German verse for about a century: see P. W. Tax, *Notker der Deutsche, Boethius, 'De consolatione Philosophiae' Buch II/I* (Altdeutsche Textbibliothek, 94; Tübingen, 1986), pp. xliii–xliv, with references.

Quę sitio votis. nunc
oscula porrigat oris,
Quę mihi venturu[m] p[ro]mp
sere organa vatu[m].
Nunc etia[m] p[er] se prę
sens dignetur adesse.
Oscula prębendo. sua
dulcia verba loquendo.
Ubera nempe tui prę
cellunt pocula vini.
Suaviter unguentis fra
grantia sat preciosis.
Mitificans veterem tua
lenis gr[ati]a legem.
Gratis iustificat quos
lex punire iubebat.
Hosq[ue] tuis donis dum
spiritualiter unguis.
Reddunt preclaram post
turpia crimina famam.

Sponse tuu[m] nomen
olei p[er]dulce liquamen.
Quod se dilatat. dum
largo nectare manat.
Gr[ati]a non stillat. sed et
ipsa voce redundat.
X[rist]icolę dicti nam
sunt de nomine x[rist]i.
Inde places teneris tu
dulcis sponse puellis.
Scilicet una salus in te

OSCULET[ur] me osculo oris sui.

QUIA meliora s[un]t ubera tua vino. fragrantia unguentis optimis.

OLEUM effusum nomen tuum.

IDEO adolescen

Cusser mih mit demo cusse sines mundes. Dicco gehiezzer mir sine cuonft p[er] p[ro]phetas. nu cume er selbo. unte cusse mih mit dero suozze sines euangelii.

Wanta bezzer sint dine spunne demo wine. sie stinchente. mit den bezzesten salbon. Div suozze dinero gr[ati]e. ist bezzera. danne div scarfe dero legis. als iz quit. lex p[er] moysen data e[st]. gr[ati]a et veritas p[er] i[esu]m x[ristu]m facta e[st]. Div selba genada ist gemisket mit variis donis sp[iritu]s s[an]c[t]i. mit den du machost ex peccatoribus iustos. ex da[m]nandis remunerandos.

Din namo. ist ul gegozzenaz ole. Din namo. ist witeno gebreitet. wanta vone dir x[rist]o. heizzen wir x[rist]iani.

Vone div minnont dih. die iunkfrouvon. daz sint die sela. dieder

D. MONASTIC BIBLES

13. The Stavelot Bible: London, British Library, MSS Add. 28106–28107, here MS 28107, fol. 163r.
a. 1097: Stavelot (dioc. Liège).

A page from the most precisely documented of all the great Romanesque Bibles. Goderann and Ernesto, monks of Stavelot, wrote, illuminated and bound this two-volume Bible between 1093 and 1097.

Parchment; (I) 230 fol.; page 580 x 380 mm.; text 446 x 270/280 mm.; column 446 x 120 mm.; 52 lines. (II) 241 + ix fol.; page 580 x 380 mm.; text 446 x 280 mm.; column 446 x 120 mm.; 53 lines. Both volumes are ruled in pencil, often erased, with wide double boundary-lines on the outside. Dimensions, ruling and *mise-en-page* are identical in both volumes; the script is a large, steady late Carolingian minuscule. Volume II has a fine full-page miniature and canon-tables. Each book of the Bible is preceded by a list of *capitula,* and begins with a high-quality historiated initial, generally showing the author of the book or an event within the text, here Zacharias struck dumb (Luke 1:5–22, at 20).

Each volume ends with a colophon identifying Goderann and Ernesto as the makers of the Bible, their abbot, Rudolf of Stavelot, and their bishop, Otbert of Liège:

> . . . These two manuscripts were written without interruption and indeed laboriously for the best part of four years. That was what it took to complete them: the writing, the illumination and the binding. Both were finished in the same year, though volume II was finished before volume I (Add. 28106, fol. 228r; similar colophon at Add. 28107, fol. 240r).

No other craftsmen are mentioned. Goderann and Ernesto had the overall responsibility, and no doubt the lion's share of the work. But how did they divide the labor? Goderann already had the experience of writing the Lobbes Bible of 1084, when he was a monk of that house.[1] A decade later he had moved to Stavelot, another great monastic house in the diocese of Liège.[2] Given that the Stavelot and Lobbes Bibles were entirely written by the same scribe (Gilissen), we must infer that Ernesto's part was to orchestrate the illumination. He is reasonably identified with 'the master of the Minor Prophets' (Dynes, pp. 80–83); four colleagues appear from time to time throughout the two volumes. The assumption that one of the illuminators was Goderann (Cahn, p. 130) seems to arise from the stylistic coincidence of some of these initials with those in the Lobbes Bible. If the comparison is valid, then the scribe Goderann is acting as an artist in his own text (Alexander, Cohen-Mushlin). But nowhere in the elaborate colophons is Goderann described as an illuminator, rather he was a monk whose 'labor' consisted in writing texts: 'Codices hi ambo quia continuatim et tamen morosius scripti sunt per annos ferme iiii^{or}'.[3]

Bibliography: J. J. G. Alexander, *The Decorated Letter* (London, 1978); Cahn, pp. 126–36 and 265, and figs. 83, 85 (both color) and 86–88; A. Cohen-Mushlin, *The Making of a Manuscript: The Worms Bible of 1148* (Wiesbaden, 1983); W. Dynes, *The Illumination of the Stavelot Bible* (New York/London, 1978); L. Gilissen, *L'expertise des écritures médiévales* (Ghent, 1973), pp. 65–75 and pl. 7; F. Masai, 'Les manuscrits à peintures de Sambre et Meuse aux XIe et XIIe siècles', *Cahiers de civilisation médiévale* 3 (1960) 169–89; F. Masai and M. Wittek, *Manuscrits datés conservés en Belgique 1:819–1400* (Brussels/Ghent, 1968), no. 2 and pll. 3–7; Watson, *British Library,* no. 321, pp. 70–71, pl. 52.

---

[1] Masai, p. 177: 'ego peccator Goderannus, professione . . . monachus . . . labore manuum mearum desudaui in sancta tua ecclesia quam . . . in lobiensi coenobio . . . fieri voluisti'.

[2] See the end of the colophon to volume II: 'Rodulfo nostro abbate'.

[3] Stavelot Bible, vol. I, fol. 228rb. The MS does read 'quia'.

XIII Quaerit quomodo xpc filius sit dauid cum dns ab eo uocetur in psal
mo centesimo nono. elationem qq: scribarum arguit. uiduam in
gazophilaciū duo era mittentem plus omib' misisse confirmat·

XIIII Laudantibus aedificium templi predicit ocius destruendum. & inter
rogantibus de fine respondit mala plurima precessura. nec precogi
tandum quid traditi loquantur sed in patientia
sua possideant animas suas·

XV Circumdandam ab exercitu hierusalem. & ue pregnantibus. gladium
quoq: & captiuitatem signa q: celi futura. seq: uenturum in nube cum
potestate magna & maiestate predicit·

VI Respicite inquit quia appropinquat redemptio urā. ab ebrietate qq: &
curis huius uite prohibens. uigilandum precipit & orandum·

VII Iudas paciscitur precium cum iudeis. parant discipuli pascha.
mysterium cene dominice celebratur·

VIII Contentionem discipulorum seipsum illorum ministrum astruens
tollit. qb' regnū pmittens ait p' aliqua petro. confirma frs tuos·

IIII Passionis gesta narrantur. ubi int cetera etiam auriculam quam
puero petrus absciderat ipse manus sue tactu restituit·

Crucifigentibus ueniam a patre deposcens. etiam unum
ex latronibus crucifixum confitentem absoluit·

Resurrexisse eum mulieres angelica reuelatione cognoscunt. & pe
trus ad monumentū currens & uidens qd factū fuerat ammiratur·

II A duobus id est cleopa & socio eius cuius nomen tacetur euntib' in
castellum qd tunc emmaus uocabatur post confabula
tionem prolixam in fractione panis agnoscitur·

Colloquentibus discipulis astans in medio dicit pax uobis. & adhuc
pauentes spiritumq: putantes ostensione transfixarum manuum
pedumq: confirmat. edens coram ipsis partem piscis assi & fauum
mellis instruit eos. promissum patris missurum se dicens
ascendit in celum· EXPLICIUNT CAPITULA·

INCIPIT EUANGELIUM SCDM LUCAM:

NIAM QUIDEM
multi conati sunt ordinare
narrationem que in nobis complete sunt
rerum. sicut tradiderunt nobis qui ab initio
ipsi uiderunt & ministri fuerunt sermonis.
uisum est & mihi assecuto a principio omnibus
diligenter ex ordine tibi scribere optime theo
phile. ut cognoscas eorum uerborum de quibus
eruditus es ueritatem· II.
Fuit in diebus herodis regis iudee sacerdos qui
dam nomine zacharias de uice abia. & uxor illi
de filiabus aaron. & nomen eius elisabeth· Erant
autem iusti ambo ante dm̄. incedentes in omnib'
mandatis & iustificationibus dnī sine querela·
Et non erat illis filius. eo quod esset elisabeth steri
lis. & ambo processissent in diebus suis· Factum
est autem cum sacerdotio fungeretur zacharias in ordine
uicis sue ante dm̄. scdm consuetudinem sacerdotii
sorte exiit ut incensum poneret ingressus in tem
plum dnī· Et omnis multitudo erat populi.
orans foris hora incensi· Apparuit autem illi an
gelus dnī. stans a dextris altaris incensi· Et za
charias turbatus est uidens. & timor irruit super
eum· Ait autem ad illum angls· Ne timeas za
charia. quoniam exaudita est deprecatio tua·
Et uxor tua elisabeth pariet tibi filium. & uoca
bis nomen eius iohannem· Et erit gaudium tibi
& exultatio. & multi in natiuitate eius gaudebūt·
Erit enim magnus coram dno. & uinum & siceram
non bibet· Et spū sco replebitur adhuc ex utero
matris sue. & multos filiorum isrl conuertet ad
dnm̄ dm̄ ipsorum· Et ipse precedet ante illum in
spū & uirtute helie. ut conuertat corda patrū in
filios & incredibiles ad prudentiam iustorum. pa
rare dno plebem perfectam· Et dixit zacharias
ad angl̄m· Unde hoc sciam? Ego enim sum senex.
& uxor mea processit in diebus suis· Et respondens
angls dixit ei· Ego sum gabriel qui asto ante
dm̄. & missus sum loqui ad te. & hec tibi euangeli
zare· Et ecce eris tacens. & non poteris loqui usq:
in diem quo hec fiant. pro eo quod non credidisti
uerbis meis que implebuntur in tempore suo·
Et erat plebs expectans zachariam. & miraban
tur quod tardaret ipse in templo· Egressus autē
non poterat loqui ad illos. & cognouerunt quod
uisionem uidisset in templo· Et ipse erat innuens
illis. & permansit mutus· Et factum est ut im
pleti sunt dies officii eius. abiit in domum suam·
Post hos autem dies concepit elisabeth uxor eius.
& occultabat se mensibus quinq: dicens· Quia sic
mihi fecit dns. in diebus quibus respexit auferre
opprobrium meum inter homines· III.
In mense autem sexto missus est angls gabriel a
dō in ciuitatem galilee cui nomen nazareth ad
uirginem desponsatam uiro cui nomen erat ioseph
de domo dauid. & nomen uirginis maria· Et in
gressus angelus ad eam dixit· Aue gratia plena.
dns tecum· Benedicta tu in mulieribus· Quae

14. The Glossed Bible: Oxford, Bodleian Library, MS Auct. D.1.13, fol. 1r. s. $xii^{med.}$: ?Winchester.

The opening page to a text of the fourteen Pauline Epistles with the *Glossa ordinaria.* The mid-twelfth-century date reflects the major initial *P* rather than the text as a whole. The conservative *mise-en-page* suggests a date distinctly before 1150.

Parchment; vi + 154 fol.; quires i–xviii^{8}, xix^{10}; page 297 x 192 mm.; text 208 x 79 mm.; text and gloss 208 x 165 mm.; 21 lines (text). Ruled with a stylus throughout (except quire xviii). Binding of tawed leather *c.* 1600, on older boards. The whole volume has been seriously weakened by damp. English, perhaps Winchester (Pächt and Alexander 3.130); acquired by Exeter cathedral (1506 catalogue), whence to the newly founded Bodleian Library, Oxford in 1602. In the late eighteenth century the manuscript was exhibited in the Auctarium, an upper solar room in the Bodleian—whence its *Auct.* shelf-mark (*SC* 1, pp. xxxix–xl).

The fine historiated initial contains scenes from the life of St. Paul (Eleen): disputing; being lowered from the walls of Damascus (Dinkler-von Schubert); martyrdom. Such scenes were current also in fresco (St. Paul and the Viper: Canterbury Cathedral) and enamel (e.g. St. Paul disputing: Victoria and Albert Museum). Here the high quality of the figure-drawing and its stylistic similarity to a contemporary initial at Mont St. Michel suggests that a professional artist was called in to draw this one opening initial. Another, perhaps local, painter colored it according to his instructions: r(ouge), v(ert) and a(zure); see the color plate and details in de Hamel, *History,* p. 105 and pll. 97–98. The A of PAVLVS, and the initials at the beginning of each subsequent Epistle, are in an older style that is very common in English monastic illumination.

The page was ruled, the initial drawn, the text and gloss written and finally the rubrication added (Incipit . . . AVLVS). Text and gloss are by the same scribe, a man whose modest latinity, or inattention, allowed him two errors in the first four lines of text. The marginal gloss is at approximately half-spacing to the text; the interlinear gloss is in two tiers: thus (text lines 6–8) the gloss 'Secundum quod homo . . . cum patre per' continues 'unionem verbi' below, while the gloss 'Vel probet filius . . . remis' continues 'sione peccatorum'. The marginal gloss has drawn on various authors, sometimes named, as AMBR(osius), and in principle identified by the number of horizontal strokes in the paraph signs. Thus the next quotation from 'Ambrose' also has a two-stroke paraph sign, at 'Congaudet'.

Bibliography: *SC* 2.2098; *Ambrosiastri qui dicitur commentarius in Epistolas Paulinas pars prima in epistolam ad Romanos,* ed. H. J. Vogels (CSEL, 81; Vienna, 1966), here at pp. 16–23; K. Froehlich and M. T. Gibson, *Biblia latina cum Glossa ordinaria* (Louvain, 1992). E. Dinkler-von Schubert, *'Per murum dimiserunt eum:* zur Ikonographie von Acts IX,25 und 2.Cor. XI,33' in *Studien zur Buchmalerei und Goldschmiedekunst des Mittelalters: Festschrift für Karl Hermann Usener zum 60. Geburtstag am 19. August 1965,* ed. F. Dettweiler et al. (Marburg-ander Lahn, 1967), pp. 79–92; L. Eleen, *The Illustration of the Pauline Epistles in French and English Bibles of the Twelfth and Thirteenth Centuries* (Oxford, 1982); C. F. R. de Hamel, *Glossed Books of the Bible and the Origins of the Paris Booktrade* (Woodbridge, 1984); *A History of Illuminated Manuscripts* (Oxford, 1986); C. M. Kauffmann, *Romanesque Manuscripts, 1066–1190* (A Survey of Manuscripts Illuminated in the British Isles, 3; London, 1975); R. M. Thomson, *Manuscripts from St. Albans Abbey, 1066–1235,* 2 vols. (Woodbridge, 1982).

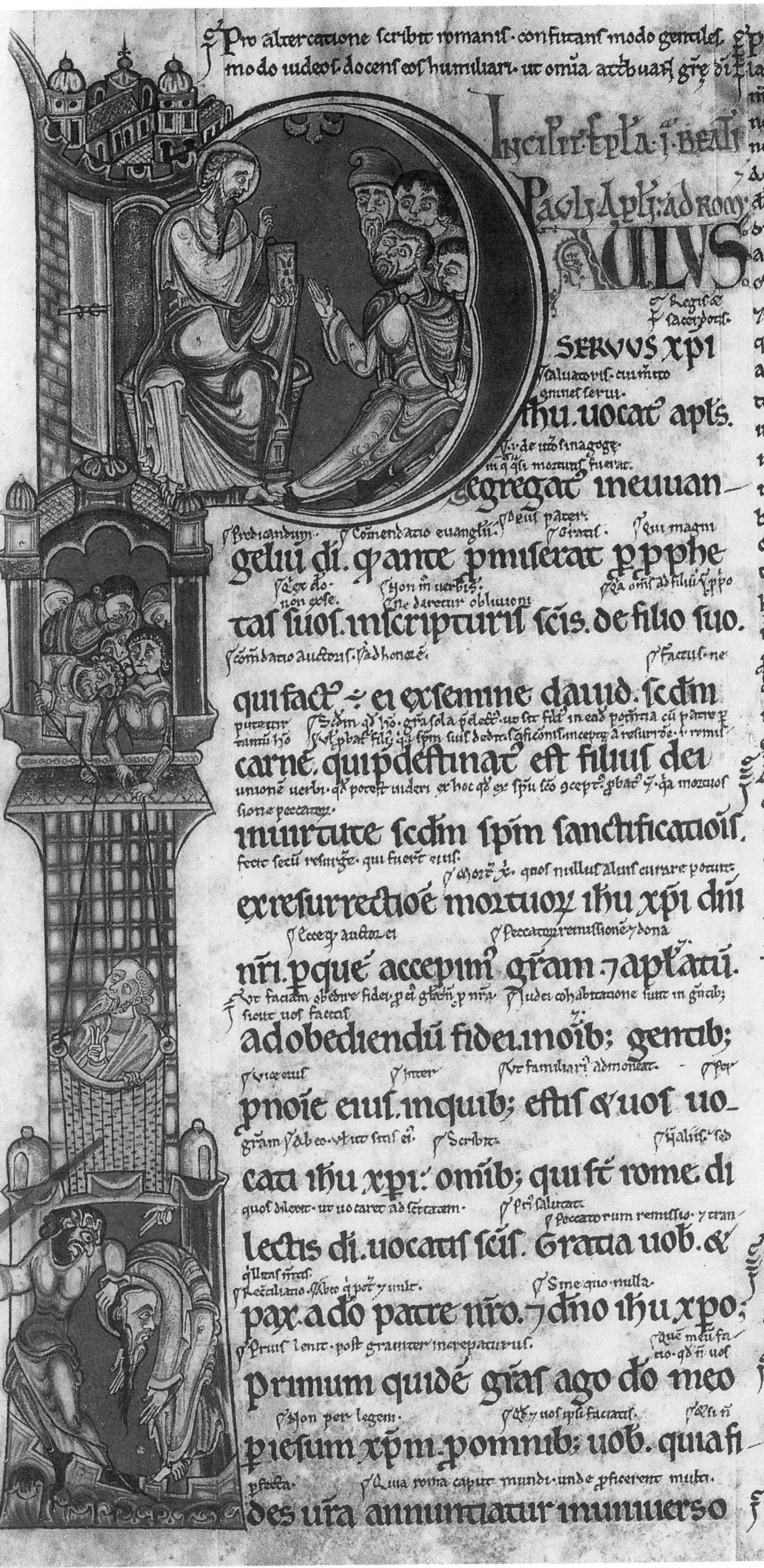

Incipit ep̄la .i. beati Pauli ap̄li ad Rom

PAULUS

SERVUS XPI

IHU. UOCAT' AP̄LS.

SEGREGAT' IN EUUAN-

GELIŪ DI. Q ANTE PMISERAT P PPHE-

TAS SUOS. IN SCRIPTURIS SCIS. DE FILIO SUO.

QUI FACT' Ē EI EX SEMINE DAUID. SCDM

CARNĒ. QUI PDESTINAT' EST FILIUS DEI

IN UIRTUTE SCDM SPM SANCTIFICATIOIS.

EX RESURRECTIOĒ MORTUOR IHU XPI DNI

NRI. P QUĒ ACCEPIM GRAM ET AP̄LATŪ.

AD OBEDIENDŪ FIDEI. IN OĪB; GENTIB;

PNOĪE EIUS. IN QUIB; ESTIS & UOS UO-

CATI IHU XPI. OMIB; QUI SŪT ROME. DI-

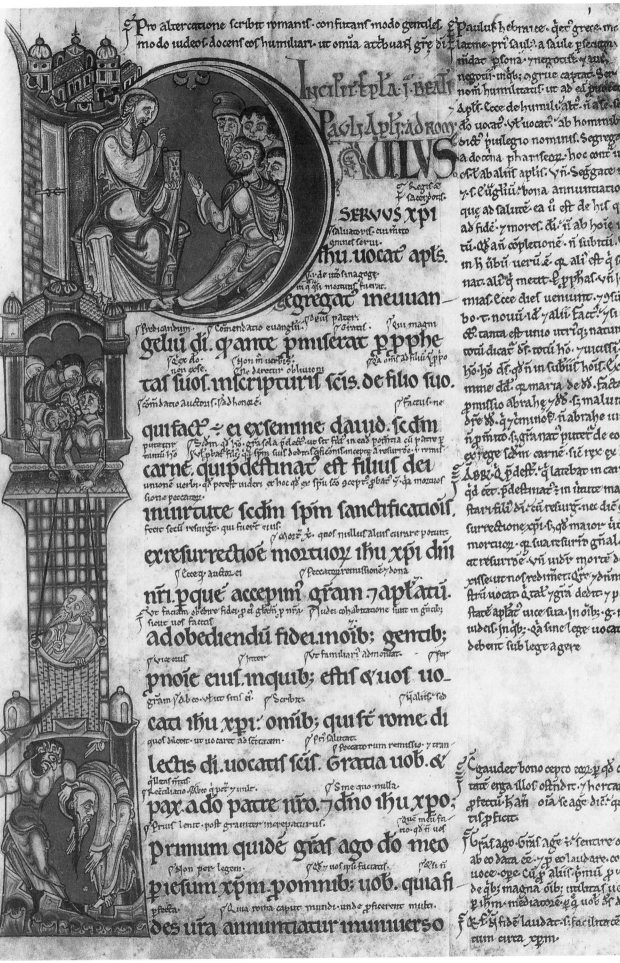

LECTIS DI. UOCATIS SCIS. GRATIA UOB. &

PAX A DO PATRE NRO. ET DNO IHU XPO.

PRIMUM QUIDĒ GRAS AGO DO MEO

P IESUM XPM. P OMNIB; UOB. QUIA FI-

DES URA ANNUNTIATUR IN UNIUERSO

15. Nicholas of Lyra OFM, 'Postillae' on the Bible: Oxford, Bodleian Library, MS Bodley 251, fol. 120r. s. xiv4/4

A century of scholastic theology and a considerable advance in the study of foreign languages were two factors (perhaps not the only two) which put a question-mark over the traditional exegesis of the Fathers, the Carolingians and the twelfth-century monastic and secular commentators. The *Postillae litterales* of Nicholas of Lyra are based on a working knowledge of Hebrew, a familiarity with Jewish exegesis and—most important—a clear distinction between the literal meaning of the text and any further construction that may be put upon it. They offered the student a solid base for both inquiry and devotion. Like Rabanus, Nicholas covered the entire Bible and his commentary too became a classic: The *Postillae* ran into over a hundred printed editions between 1472 and 1600 (**no. 16**). There is no modern edition.

Parchment; page 458 x 323 mm.; text 320 x 207 mm.; column 320 x 94 mm.; 69 lines. Decoration: French, full foliate borders, with gold, at the beginning of each book of the Bible.

Bodley 251 is the first volume (Genesis–Ecclesiasticus) of a massive library edition of the *Postillae,* that was owned—and doubtless commissioned—by William Courtenay, archbishop of Canterbury (1381–96).[1] Each chapter begins with a three-line initial in red or blue with contrasting penwork flourishing. Paraph signs in red or blue divide the chapters internally. The *lemmata* from the text of the Bible are underlined in red. At the top of each page is a running heading in alternating red and blue capitals, here RVTH.

The passage shown here includes Ruth 1:15–16, 'Intreat me not to leave thee, nor to return from following after thee: for whither thou goest I will go; and where thou lodgest I will lodge: thy people shall be my people, and thy God my God' (col. 1, lines 19–29). Nicholas explains not that Ruth 'is' the Gentiles, but that as a Moabite she was non-Jewish; so it was a total denial of her family and culture to go with her mother-in-law, live among the Jews, and accept their God. Yet by doing so she became a link in the genealogical chain from Adam to Christ (Ruth 4:13–22).

Bibliography: *SC* 2332; Pächt and Alexander 1.614.

[1]The second volume (Isaiah–Apocalypse) has not been identified.

filijs et diuicijs. Non aut est verisile quod rex moab de
disset filiam suam vxorem vno pauperi et extraneo. et si post
mortem depauperatus fuisset vir eius: non est verisile quod p
mulieres eam recedere de terra sua ita paup: quod indiget
colligere spicas in agro. sicut dicitur de ruth secundo ca. et io
mag. vr. quod ipsa ruth fuit de ignobili plebe, sequitur. Audierat
enim etc. et ideo fame recedente de terra sua: melius potuit
ad eam redire. Ite in domum matris vestre. hoc dicit quia
patres earum erant mortui: vel quia mulieres sunt magis fami
liares matribus suis quam patribus. Que eleuata voce fle
re ceperunt etc. ex quo patet quod noemi se valde bñ habuerat
ad nurus suas. non ultra habeo filios in vtero meo ut
viros ex me sperare possitis. precepti enim erat in lege.
Deut. xxv. ~~xxv~~ c. quod si aliquis moreretur sine herede re
licta vxore: frater eius acciperet eam ad suscitandum semen fratri
defuncto. Cetera patent in littera. ¶ Cui dixit noemi. hic
consequenter declaratur ipsius ruth constancia que noluit reuerti sic
aliter. sed ire ad terram israel cum socru sua et conuerti ad cultum
vnius dei gentilitate relicta. propter quod dixit. ne aduerseris
mihi: ut relinquam te et abeam. reuertendo ad cultum ydolorum.
Quocumque perrexeris etc. hic dicunt hebrei quod uolentibus conuerti
ad iudaismum: dicenda sunt grauia legis secundum partem sicut uolens
tibi ingredi religionem explicanda sunt difficilia illius
religionis. dicunt ergo quod noemi videns ruth uelle conuerti
ad iudaismum. dixit sibi aliqua onera legis et primo dixit
ei quod non erat licitum iudeis ne exire terram israel nisi ex
causa magne necessitatis. et tunc Ruth ei respondit. quocumque
perrexeris pergam. et ubi abieris. Item dixit ei. Non est
nobis licitum quod mulier sit cum viro nisi fuit maritus eius.
Et ruth respondit. vbi morata fueris et ego pariter morabor.
nolens esse sine te cum aliquo viro. Item dixit. populus
hebreorum est astrictus legis oneribus in quibus sunt .dc.xiij.
precepta. tunc respondit. populus meus populus tuus. q.d. volo subdi
legi ipsius. ¶ Item dixit prohibitum est nobis colere deos
alienos. et ipsa respondit. deus tuus deus meus. q.d. alium
nolo colere. Item dixit ei. transgressoribus legis nostre in di
uersis casibus imponitur pena quadruplicis mortis. scilicet la
pidacionis. combustionis. strangulacionis in suspensione: et
occisionis gladio. ut patet in exo. et deutro. et tunc Ruth respon
dit. que te terra susceperit moriente et in ea moriar. q.d.
parata sum suscipere penam cuiuscumque mortis si meruero
sicut et tu. videns ergo noemi etc. quia qui aliquis est firma
voluntate transeundi ad legem diuinam uel religionem: non est im
pediendus seu retrahendus. cetera patent usque ibi. Dicebant
que mulieres hec est illa noemi. secundum expositores nostros. legi
tur positiue. et est verbum causa gaudendi de reditu noemi.
Secundum hebreos vero legitur interrogatiue et est verbum admiracionis.
quasi dicatur. hec est illa noemi que recessit cum viro et
cum filiis et diuiciis. et modo reuertitur paup et peregrinando. quia ex
iuit terram israel ex mala causa. ut supradictum est secundum opio
nem hebreorum. et huic consonat quod sequitur. Egressa sum plena. fi
lijs et diuicijs. et vacuam reduxit me dominus. et in hoc confitetur
penam sibi inflictam a domino pro peccato suo exitus de terra israel
ex mala causa. ut supradictum est secundum opinionem hebreorum .ij. cap.

¶ Erat autem. hic consequenter describitur ipsius Ruth conuersacio
virtuosa. et quia humilitas est fundamentum omnium vir
tutum. ideo circa eam post describitur humilitatis virtus
secundo honestatis decus ibi. accidit autem. Tercio gratitudo
in beneficijs ibi. Que cadens in faciem suam. Quarto sollicitu
do in exercicijs ibi. Collegit ergo. humilitas autem eius ap
paret in hoc quod optulit se ad colligendum spicas in agro de
voluntate et licencia socrus sue: primum. hic tamen nomen ipsius
booz eo quod ager in quo collegit erat ipsius qui et erat
de cognacione mariti sui defuncti. et hoc est quod dicitur. Erat autem
vir elimelech consanguineus. dicunt hebrei quod elimelech socer Ruth. et salmon
pater booz. fuerunt fratres. et secundum hoc maritus Ruth et booz erant
consanguinei germani. sed primum decet verisimilius. quia salmon qui
genuit booz de raab fuit tempore Josue. et accepit vxorem

raab post destructionem vrbis iericho. quia tunc fuit copulata
populo israel. ut habetur Josue. vj. hoc autem fuit circa principium ducatus
Josue. a principio vero ducatus eius usque ad abesan qui iudex dicitur
autem est ipsum booz fluxerunt anni .cc. lxxij. et multo plures
fuerunt usque ad heli. et ideo secundum opinionem hebreorum dicatur quod booz
et abesan idem hic fuit. impossibile videtur quod elimelech fuerit frater sal
mon. quia ruth vxor maalon filii elimelech adhuc erat iu
uenis ut satis patet ex sequentibus quando fuit copulata matrimonio
ipsi booz adhuc potentia generare. adhuc magis est impossibile hoc imo
quod booz fuit tempore heli qui post eam per multos annos iudicauit.
propter quod dicunt doctores nostri et verius ut videtur quod tres fuerunt booz sibi
succedentes. quorum primus fuit auus. secundus filius. tercius nepos.
primus fuit filius salmon qui genuit de raab. et tercius fuit iste
qui genuit ephod obed ex ruth. et hoc ideo dixi secundum mathiam
po. ca. quod isti tres sub vno nomine comprehenduntur. tamen quia completur
dicitur eodem modo in fine huius libri sub vno nomine. cum ma
theus euangelista genealogiam saluatoris in tribus quaternarijs
voluit describere. ut ibidem dicitur. In quo autem gradu vterque booz
attinebat ipsi elimelech et filio eius mahalon: post eam di
cetur. Cetera patent in littera. ¶ accidit autem. hic describitur
ipsius Ruth honestatis decus. quod percepit booz ueniens ad
messores suos. vnde subditur. Dixitque booz iuueni qui messo
ribus preerat cuius est hec puella. secundum quod dicunt hebrei. et satis apparet
ex textu. booz iam erat homo prouecte etatis et honora
bilis bone fame et virtutis, et ideo non est verisile quod quereret de
aliqua iuuencula nisi que esset in bone honestatis signaculis
quam in ea videret. et ideo dicunt hebrei quod spicas stantes post mes
sores colligebat stando, iacentes autem colligebat sedendo
ne inclinando se ad colligendum: uestes sue eleuarentur et aperte
posterior. et post aliqua tibiarum suarum discooperta appareret. et
ideo booz videns eius honestatem: motus fuit ad querendum
que esset et ad faciendum sibi graciam. dicens ei quod sequitur. Audi filia.
etc. et patet littera. patet et quod erat iuuencula ex ipsius quia vocauit eam
filiam. ¶ Que cadens in faciem suam etc. hic commendatur Ruth
de gratitudine. quia ipsi booz de beneficijs oblatis licet non essent
multum magna valde fuit regraciata. et patet littera usque ibi. que non
sum similis vnius puellarum tuarum. In hebreo habetur. ancillarum tuarum
q.d. non sum tanti valoris sicut minima ancilla tua. et ideo
maiorem graciam inueni apud ipsum booz. vnde subditur. dixit quia
ad eam booz. quando hora vescendi fuit. veni huc et comede
panem. i. cibum paratum de domo mea cum famulis meis. et
intinge bucellam tuam in aceto. acetum enim multum refrigerat
et ideo in calidis regionibus cuiusmodi est terra israel. vtuntur
aceto. maxime tempore calido cuiusmodi est tempus messionis
et congessit polentam sibi. i. ipsa Ruth preparauit sibi cibum secundum
consuetudinem suam. In hebreo habetur. porrexit ei graciam. i. cibum
factum de granis nouis. que de manu sua dedit booz ipsi Ruth. ut
dicunt hebrei. Cetera patent in littera. ¶ Collegit etc. hic conse
quenter describitur sollicitudo ipsius ruth. in opere pro quo ueniebat de volun
tate socrus sue. cum dicitur. Collegit ergo in agro usque ad vesperam.
et excuciens inuenit ordei quasi mensuram ephi. quod autem dicitur. i.
tres modios. non est in hebreo. sed loco eius habetur ordeorum. quia inuenit
ephi ordei in hoc quod collegerat. cuius autem quantitatis sit hec mensura
que vocatur ephi: dictum fuit exo. xvj. gomor enim est decima pars ephi
et gomor ~~enim est decima pars ephi~~ manne sufficiebat vnius diei
pro una persona. ut ibidem dicitur. Juxta est ita quod puellis booz. i. ancillis. cetera patent in littera. Tercium capitulum.

¶ Postquam autem. hic consequenter describitur coniugium ruth cum booz secundum legem
que habetur. Deut. xxv. de suscitacione seminis
defuncti: ipsa requirebat booz de matrimonio de consilio socrus
sue. et ideo circa hoc primo ponitur socrus consultacio. Secundo nurus
obtemperacio. Tercio ipsius booz racionabilis responsio. Secunda ibi. Que
respondit. Tercia ibi. Et ille. Circa primum dicitur. postquam autem reuersa
est ad socrum suam. i. de messionibus quarum tempore fuerat coniuncta
puellis booz. ut dictum est in fine precedentis capituli. Queram tibi requiem
i. matrimonium bonum: ita quod non oporteat te laborare pro victu.
Et prouideo ut bene sit tibi. hic ideo ponitur quia maxime desiderant mulieres.
Ista hac nocte aream ordei ventilat. i. festum facit pro
ventilacione. dicunt enim aliqui quod mos erat antiquorum in ven

16. The 'Glossa ordinaria' with the Literal Postills of Nicholas of Lyra, printed by Paganinus de Paganinis: Oxford, Bodleian Library, Auct.V.Q.inf.II.6, fol. 279r (Venice, 1495).

The early printers found their markets not primarily in new works, nor in books for the humanist intelligentsia, but in the provision of well-tried works of reference: commentaries on civil and canon law, and Bibles, missals and choir-books for the secular and regular clergy. For example a four-volume *Glossa ordinaria* in the 1480 edition, handsomely bound, was given in 1485 by the vicar of the parish church of Kronenburg southwest of Cologne in memory of his predecessor and his family.[1] A decade later this traditional reference Bible was improved by the incorporation of Lyra's *Postills* in the lower half of each page (shown here). No sooner was this in circulation than the 1498 edition by Froben of Basel provided even more: the Bible text in the center, to the left the *Glossa ordinaria,* and Lyra's *Postills* to the right. Such combined texts quickly displaced both the *Gloss* and Lyra as independent entities.

Paper; 470 fol.; page 340 x 235 mm.; text 281 x 185 mm.; column 281 x 90 mm.; 83 lines (gloss). The Bodleian incunable belonged to St. Saviour and Holy Cross, Polling, an Augustinian house in the diocese of Augsburg. It is the first (Genesis–Esther) of four volumes, all bound in the white stamped leather on wood that is so characteristic of German monastic books of that era.

The de Paganinis edition is based on the *editio princeps* of the *Glossa ordinaria* (1480) and one or more of the editions of the *Postills* of Nicholas of Lyra: demonstrably that of Francis Renner of Heilbronn (Venice, 1482–83; BMC 5.197), and perhaps also de Paganinis's own edition of 1485 (Gosselin, pp. 408–409). His team of three editors was led by Bernardino Gadolo, a monk of S. Michele Murano, a local Camaldolese house with solid scholarly reputation.[2] Although we are thus at one remove from any manuscript of either text, a number of manuscript conventions still obtain. The book is foliated rather than paginated. The four type-sizes all reflect traditional *scriptorium* practice: (i) the running head, RVTH; (ii) the Bible text and the *lemmata* in the *Gloss;* (iii) Lyra's text; and finally (iv) the interlinear *Gloss* and the reference-letters in Lyra.[3] Another traditional device is the symbols attaching the interlinear *Gloss* to the relevant word in the text: e.g. + *agrum* is linked to + 'ecclesiam' two half-lines above. The *field* in which Ruth gleans is 'the Church'. Equally familiar is the little *e* in the margin directing the rubricator to enter a red capital E at that point by hand.

Bibliography: BMC 5.458; Goff B.608; Hain *3174; Proctor 5170. P. Glorieux, *Répertoire des maîtres en théologie de Paris au XIIIe siècle* (Études de philosophie médiévale, 18; Paris, 1934), no. 345, pp. 215–31; A. Gosselin, 'A Listing of the Printed Editions of Nicholas of Lyra', *Traditio* 26 (1970) 399–426, here no. 42, p. 410; Stegmüller, *Repertorium* 4.5829–5923, 5929–74.

[1]The *ex libris* in each volume reads (with some variants): 'Hoc uolumen cum reliquis partibus biblie glosate dominus Iohannes Gerawe huius ecclesie vicarius pro aniversali memoria pie recorde domini Iohannis Walteri altariste in Kronenburg parentumque suorum et pro participacione omnium bonorum operum ecclesie ad hanc liberariam tradidit Anno domini Mccccclxxxv' (now Princeton University, Firestone Library, EX I 5168, 1480).

[2]For Gadolo (1463–99) see *Contemporaries of Erasmus: A Biographical Register of the Renaissance and Reformation,* ed. P. Bietenholtz, 3 vols. (Toronto, 1985–88) 2.69; and for S. Michele, where the learned Pietro Delfino was his abbot and patron, see comprehensively V. Meneghin, *San Michele in Isola di Venezia,* 2 vols. (Venice, 1962) 1.168–78.

[3]For example, 'Videns ergo Noemi' (1:18) is marked with a tiny *h* above 'Videns', which identifies Lyra's comment (12 lines from the foot of the page).

ro.i.dauid relicta ⁊ a filijs.i.regibus ⁊ principib⁹ ꝓuata sterilez se esse ⁊ in firmam ad concipiendum filios deo cõfitetur post aduentum christi.

Eleuata igitur voce ⁊c. Per has mul.quarũ vna dolẽs ⁊ lugẽs a socru recedit: altera obstinato aio adheret credẽtes significant quoꝝ alij ꝑcepta gratia baptismi ⁊ societate fidei ad errores ꝓstinos relabunt: quos significat orpha.q̃ ad deos suos reuersa ẽ: alij vero definito consilio perceptã gratiaz cõsequunt quos significat ruth.

Quãdo primũ or.me.⁊c. Idest quando icarnatiõis sue ordinẽ ad mysteriũ passionis christi cõuertit: Messis eniz ordeacea tẽpus dñice passiõis exꝓmit: q̃ mẽse nouorũ.i.ꝓmo mense cõtigit. Bene ergo tẽpore illo ad bethleem veniũt qñ lex xp̃m quẽ docet in bethleẽ natũ in pascha.i. in mẽse nouoꝝ ꝑdicat occisum. Sãcta q̃z ecclesia toto nisu laborat: vt q̃s ad fidẽ cõuocat incarnationis passiõis resurrectionis merito ibuat. Messis ordeacea iudeorũ exꝓmit credulitatẽ q pacto sacramẽto passiõis ꝑdicãtibus apl̃is ꝓmũ ad fidẽ veniũt q alibi quinq̃z panibus ordeaceis pasti a domino leguntur.

Quocũq̃z.n.p.per. Si ecclia de gentib⁹ vocatã relicta patria.i.idolatria omissa carnali cõuersatiõe ⁊ desiderijs: ꝓfitetur deũ suũ eẽ in quẽ

c crediderũt sancti ⁊ iturã quo caro christi ascendit ⁊ ꝑ eius noie in hoc seculo pati vsq̃z ad mortẽ ⁊ cũ populo sanctorũ et ꝓphãrũ ⁊ patriarcharũ vñ letamini gẽtes cũ plebe eius.

Vidẽs noemi ⁊c. Gentilis ppl's obstinato animo predicatores sequit in terrã sanctã: ⁊ in ciuitatem dei bethleem: vbi ꝑparat ad suscipiendum sponsum de stirpe abrahe natũ: i quo benedicentur oẽs gentes vel tribus terre.

Nõ vocetis me ⁊c. Agnoscit synagoga calamitatẽ suã quam post aduentum christi merito

d patit ⁊ refugit pulchra vocari q̃r tpa ꝓspitatis sue finiri conspicit.

filios i utero meo: ut uiros ex me sperar possitis? Reuertimini filie mee ⁊ abite. Jam enim senectute confecta sũ: nec apta vinculo cõiugali. Etiaz si possem hac nocte cõcipe ⁊ parere filios si eos expectare uelitis donec crescãt ⁊ ãnos pubertatis ipleãt: añ eritis uetule q̃z nubatis. Nolite queso filie mee facer hoc qa ur̃a ãgustia magis ꝓmit me: ⁊ egressa ẽ mãus dñi cõtra me. Eleuata igit uoce flere rursũ cepunt: orpha osculata est socrũ ac reuersa ẽ. Ruth adhesit socrui sue. Cũi dixit noẽi: En reuersa est cognata tua ad p'lm suum: ⁊ ad deos suos: uade cũ ea. q̃ rñdit: ne aduerseris mihi ut relinquã te ⁊ abeã. Quocũq̃z eĩ prexeris pgã ⁊ ubi morata fueris: ⁊ ego pit morabor. populus tuus põpulus meus: ⁊ deus tuus deus meus. Q̃ue te t̃ra moriẽtẽ suscepit i ea moriar: ibiq̃z locũ accipiã sepulture: hec mihi faciat deus ⁊ hec addat si ñ sola mors me ⁊ te sepauerit. Uidẽns g̃ noẽi q obstinato aio ruth decreuiss secũ pgere aduersari noluit: nec ultra ad suos r̃ditũ psuader: ꝑfectiq̃z sũt sit ⁊ uenerũt i bethleẽ. Quib3 urbẽ igressis: uelox apud cũctos fama percrebruit. dicẽbãtq̃z mr'eres

h ẽ illa noẽi. Quib3 ait: Ne uocetis me noẽi.i.pulchrã s3 uocate me mara hoc ẽ amarã: qa ualde amaritudie r̃pleuit me oĩpotẽs. Egressa sũ pleã: ⁊ uacuã me r̃duxit dñs: cur igr̃ uocatis me noẽi: quã dñs hũiliauit ⁊ afflixit oĩpotẽs: uẽit ergo noẽi cũ ruth moabitide nuru sua d t̃ra pegriatõis sue ac r̃uersa ẽ i bethleẽ qñ ꝓmũ hordea metebãtur. C II.

Erat autẽm uiro elimelech ꝯsanguĩeus hõ potẽs ⁊ magnaꝝ opũ noie † booz.

† ſ fortitudo dei: vnde ⁊ vocabat nomen eius ammirabilis: ꝯsiliarius: de⁹ fortis .p.p.pa.fu.seculi.

Dixitq̃z ruth moabitis ad socrũ suã: si iubes uadã i † agrũ ⁊ † colligã spicas q̃ fugerit mãus † metẽtiũ ubicũq̃z clemẽtis i me prissa miliãs r̃perero grãm. Cui illa rñdit: uad filia mea. abijt itaq̃z ⁊ colligebat spicas post t̃ga metẽtiũ. Accidit aũt ut ager ille hr̃et dñz noie booz q erat d cognatiõe elielech ⁊ ecce ipse uẽiebat de bethleẽ. Dixitq̃z messoribus: dñs uobiscũ: q rñdert ei. Bñdicat tibi dñs. † Dixitq̃z booz iuuẽi q ꝑerat messo

† ſ ecclesiã † ſ spice remanẽtes fideles significãt q trãslatis ceteri ad celũ nobis reliquunt ad exẽplum.

† ſ messis sunt sancti qui colliguntur reponendi in horreo dei. messores sunt angeli.

† ſ q̃r christus quemlibet de doctoribus q minori bus preest sacerdotibus quasi ignorãs de fide gentium sciscitat cũ eũ ꝓuocat ad predicandum

C. II.

Erat aũt viro. Vir iste cõsanguineus elimelech xp̃s est agnus legis ⁊ legislator: q̃r p legẽ ꝓmissus ⁊ de ꝓ̃iarchis nat⁹ ⁊ d gẽte iudeoꝝ s̃cd3 carnẽ. vñ: ꝓphaz suscitabit vobis de⁹ de fratrib⁹ v̈ris tãq̃z me audierit: h ẽ potẽs q mũdi ꝓncipez debellauit ⁊ totũ orbẽ suo iperio subiugauit ⁊ magnarũ opũ q̃r celi ⁊ terre possessor ẽ: ⁊ i eo sũt oẽs thesauri sapie ⁊ scie. Ipse est enim virtus dei ⁊ sapientia. a

Accidit aũt ⁊c. Q̃r scã ecclia ad xp̃m ptinet cui⁹ spõsa ⁊ corp⁹ est: de q̃ d̃r: fortitudo mea: ⁊ laus.m.do. ⁊ alibi: dñs fortis ⁊ potens .d.p.i.p. Ipse est cognatus elime

Nicolaus

Deut.xxv.q̃ si aliq̃s moreret sine herede relicta vxore: frater ei⁹ acciperet eã ad suscitãdũ semẽ fratri suo defuncto. Cetera patẽt i lr̃a. a Cui dixit noemi. Hic ꝯñr describit ipsius ruth cõuersio: q̃ noluit reuerti sicut altera: s ire ad terrã isrl' cũ socru sua ⁊ ꝯuerti ad cultũ dei vni⁹: gẽtilitate relicta: ꝓpter qd dixit: b Ne aduerseris mihi ⁊c. .reuertẽdo ad cultũ idoloꝝ. c Quocũq̃z.n.prexer ⁊c. Hic dicũt hebrei q volẽtib⁹ cõuerti ad iudaismũ dicẽda sũt grauia legis saltẽ s̃m partẽ. sicut volẽtib⁹ ingredi religionẽ explicãda sũt difficilia illi⁹ religionis. Dicunt igit q noemi vidẽs ruth velle ꝯuerti ad iudaismũ dixit sibi aliq̃ onera legis. ⁊ ꝓmo dixit ei q nõ erat licitũ iudeis ire extra terrã israel nisi ex causa magne necessitatis. ⁊ tũc ruth ei r̃ndit: Quocũq̃z prexeris pgã. ⁊ nõ alibi. Iterũ dixit ei: Nõ ẽ nobis licitum q mulier sit sola cum viro nisi fuerit maritus eius. ⁊ ruth respondit: d Ubi morata fueris ⁊c. nolẽs eẽ sine te cũ aliq̃ viro. Iterũ dixit. ppl's hebreoꝝ ẽ subiect⁹ legis onerib⁹ i. q̃ sũt sexcẽta ⁊ tredeciz ꝑcepta. Tũc rñdit: e Populus tuus ⁊c.q.d. volo subdi legi ipsius. Iterũ dixit: ꝓhibitum ẽ nobis colere deos alienos ⁊ ipa respondit: f De⁹ tu⁹ de⁹ me⁹.q.d. aliũ nolo colere. Iterũ dixit ei. trãsgressorib⁹ legis nostre i diuersis casib⁹ iponit pena q̃druplicis mortis.s. lapidatiõis: cõbustiõis: strãgulatiõis i suspensione: ⁊ occisionis gladio. vt p3 i Exodo ⁊ Deut. Et tũc ruth rñdit: g Que te terra susceperit moriẽtẽ in ea moriar.q.d. parata sum suscipere penã cuiuscũq̃z mortis si meruero sicut ⁊ tu. h Uidẽs ergo noemi ⁊c. q̃r qñ aliq̃s hẽt firmã volũtatẽ trãscẽdi ad legẽ diuinã vel religionẽ nõ ẽ ipediẽdus seu refutãd⁹. Cetera patẽt vsq̃z ibi: i Dicebãtq̃z mlieres: hec ẽ illa noemi. s̃m expositores nr̃os legit depositiue. ⁊ est verbũ cõgaudẽdi de reditu noemi. s̃m hebreos ṽo legit iterrogatiue. ⁊ est verbũ admirãdi. q̃si dicat: Hec ẽ illa noemi q̃ recessit cũ curru ⁊ eqs ⁊ diuitijs. ⁊ mõ reuertit paup ⁊ peditãdo: q̃r exiuit terraz isrl' ex mala cã: vt.s̃. dictũ est s̃m opinionẽ hebreoꝝ. ⁊ huic cõsonat quod sequitur: k Egressa sum plena. filijs ⁊ diuitijs: ⁊ vacuã me reduxit dñs. ⁊ in hoc cõfitet penã sibi inflictã a dño ꝓ pcõ sui exit⁹ de terra isrl' ex mala cã. vt.s̃. dictũ ẽ.s. s̃m opinionem hebreorum. C. II.

Erat ãt. Hic ꝯñr describit ipi⁹ ruth ꝯuersatio virtuosa. ⁊ q̃r humilitas ẽ fundamẽtũ oĩu3 ṽtutũ. iõ circa eã ꝓmo describit hu

de lyra

militatis ṽtus. secundo honestas dec⁹: ibi: Accidit aũt. tertio gratitudo i bñficijs: ibi: Que cadẽs i faciẽ suã. q̃rto sollicitudo i exercitijs: ibi: Col legit g. Humilitas autẽ ei⁹ appet i h q obtulit se ad colligẽdum spicas in agro de volũtate ⁊ licentia socrus sue: ꝓmittit t̃n h nomẽ ipsi⁹ booz: eo q ager in quo collegit erat ipsi⁹: q ẽt erat de cognatiõe mariti sui defuncti. ⁊ h ẽ qd d̃r: Erat ãt viro elimelech ꝯsanguineus. Dicũt hebrei q elimelech socer ruth ⁊ salmõ p̃r booz fuerũt fr̃es. ⁊ sic marit⁹ ruth ⁊ booz erãt cõsãguinei germani. S3 ꝓmũ dictũ v̓r falsũ. q̃r salmõ q genuit booz de raab fuit tpe iosue. ⁊ accepit vxorẽ raab post destructionẽ vrbis hiericho. q̃r tũc fuit copulata pplo isrl'. vt h̃r Josue. vi. h ãt fuit circa ꝓncipiũ ducat⁹ iosue a ꝓncipio ṽo ducat⁹ ei⁹ vsq̃z ab abessan quẽ hebrei dicũt eẽ ip3 booz: fluxerũt ãni. cclxxij. ⁊ multo plures fluxerũt vsq̃z ad heli. ⁊ iõ si s̃m opinionem hebreoꝝ dicat q booz ⁊ abessan idẽ hõ fuit. ipossibile v̓r q elimelech fuerit frater salmon. q̃r ruth vxor maalon filij elimelech adhuc erat iuuenis. vt sat̃ p3 ex sequẽtib⁹ qñ fuit copulata matrimonio ipi booz: adhuc potẽrt generare. ⁊ adhuc magis ipossibile ẽ si dicat q booz fuit tpe heli q postea p multos annos iudicauit. pp qd dicũt doctores nostri ⁊ bñ vt v̓r q tres fuerũt booz sibi succedẽtes: quoꝝ ꝓmus fuit auus: secũdus filius: ⁊ tertius nepos. primus fuit fili⁹ salmõ quẽ genuit de raab. ⁊ terti⁹ fuit iste q genuit obed ex ruth. ⁊ hoc idẽ dixi sup Math. i. ca. vbi isti tres sub vno nomine cõprehẽdunt. tũ q̃r cõprehẽdũtur eodẽ mõ i fine hui⁹ libri sub vno noie: tũ q̃r Matheus euãgelista genealogiã saluatoris i trib⁹ quaterdenis voluit describere: vt ibidẽ d̓r. i quo ãt gradu vltimus booz attinebat ipi elimelech ⁊ filio ei⁹ maalon: postea dicet. Cetera patẽt in lr̃a. m Accidit autem. Hic describit ipsius ruth honestas dec⁹ qd pcepit booz veniẽs ad messores suos. vñ subdit: n Dixitq̃z booz iuueni q messorib⁹ preerat ⁊c. F3 q dicũt hebrei ⁊ satis apparet ex textu. booz iã erat homo ꝓuecte etatis ⁊ honorabilis rõne sciẽtie ⁊ virtutis. ⁊ iõ nõ est verisimile q q̃reret de aliq̃ iuuẽcula muliere q̃ eẽt: nisi rõne honestatis singularis quã i ea videret. et iõ dicũt hebrei q spicas stãtes remanẽtes post messores colligebat stando. iacẽtes aũt colligebat sedẽdo: ne iclinãdo se ad colligẽdũ vestes sue eleuarẽtur a pte posteriori: ⁊ pars aliqua tibiaꝝ suarũ discooperta appareret. ⁊ ideo booz vidẽs ei⁹ honestatẽ mot⁹ fuit ad q̃rẽdũ q̃ eẽt ⁊ ad faciendu3 sibi B

E. THE UNIVERSITY TEXT

17. Peter Lombard, 'Magna Glosatura' on the Pauline Epistles: Oxford, Bodleian Library, MS Bodley 725, fol. 10r. s. xii$^{ex.}$: Exeter Cathedral.

The *Magna glosatura* is so called by comparison with the *Parva glosatura* attributed to Anselm of Laon (**no. 14**) and the *Media glosatura* of Gilbert de la Porrée. In combining extensive, and sourced, quotation from the Fathers with 'modern' analysis of the argument, Peter Lombard has created a commentary which owes something to the choice of authors in the *Parva glosatura* and a little to the rhetorical example of the *Media glosatura*, but which is essentially new.

Parchment; v + 311 fol.; page 349 x 237 mm.; text 227 x 150 mm.; 42 lines. Ruled in pencil, with double vertical boundary-lines to right and left of the main text and on the outer edge of the Bible text (all *c.* 6 mm.). The column of references (27 mm.) is delimited by single red boundary-lines with ornamental tails. Fine initials with mythical beasts (e.g. centaur, fol. 202v: Alexander) to the Lombard's preface to Romans and at the beginning of each Epistle. *Lemmata* underlined in red, and references written in red; no further decoration. No chapter-divisions. With its companion volume Bodleian MS Auct. D.2.8, Peter Lombard on the Psalms, this manuscript was in Exeter Cathedral throughout the later Middle Ages (Pächt and Alexander).

Romans 1:5–6 (text) and 1:3–4 (commentary: *PL* 191:1307B–1309B). As the text is provided in full within the commentary, the column on the extreme left here is superfluous and indeed nearly useless; it reflects the desire to convert a continuous commentary into a formal glossed text. Other contemporary manuscripts of the Lombard's commentary offer various solutions to the same problem: the text from time to time in a larger script in the main body of the page; a narrow central column of text or gloss; outer columns with gloss only; Herbert of Bosham's *de luxe* folio glossed text with his own editorial additions and emendations.[1] The Lombard normally quotes his sources *verbatim.* They are identified in the outer margin by a system of dots that could work much better than it does in the present manuscript. Here the three-dot Ambrose (line 16) correlates correctly with 'Sciendum tamen' (line 15), the dot-and-comma (line 24) with 'Querens' (line 24) and the triple apostrophe (line 26) with 'propter' (line 25); but all the other passages have either a two-dot reference or none at all. Other notes concern the rhetorical structure of Paul's text: here 'Intende' (line 38), elsewhere 'questio', 'responsio', 'ratio' and the like.

Bibliography: *PL* 191:1297–192:520; *SC* 2654. J. J. G. Alexander, *The Decorated Letter* (London, 1978), fig. xvii (fol. 202v: detail); M. Colish, *Peter Lombard* (forthcoming); Pächt and Alexander, 3.232.

[1] See respectively Oxford, Bodleian Library, MS Rawl. G. 165 (larger script), MS Rawl. G. 171 (central column) and Cambridge, Trinity College, MSS B.5.6-7 (Herbert of Bosham).

accepi-
mus
grati-
am &
apo-
stola-
tum
adobe-
dien-
dum
fidei
inom-
nib;
genti-
bus
pro-
nomi-
ne ei.
inqui-
bus
& uos

nā hōis s; natam. Cūq; tota trinitas opata sit formationē suscepti hōis. qm inseparabilia sc̄ opa
trinitatis: solus tn̄ filius accep hoīem .i. formā serui in singularitate siue in unitate p̄. ñ in unitate seu ī singularitate diuine nature. Si aūt adhuc qrit̄ ipsa incarnatio qm̄ fc̄a sit ipm̄ ūbū
di dico carnē fcm̄ .i. hoīem fcm̄ ñ tn̄ in h q̄ fcm̄ ē ūsum atq; mutatū: s; carne ut car-
nalib; ɔgruent̄ appareret indutū. Ita sane fcm̄ ut ibi sit ñ tm̄ ūbū dī 7 hōis caro: s; 7 rōnal
hōis aīa atq; h totū 7 ds̄ dicat̄ pp̄ dm̄. 7 hō pp̄ hoīem. Agnoscam̄ g̃ geminā subam x̄.
diuinā .s. q̄ eqlis ē pr̄i. 7 humanā q̄ maior ē pat̄ utrūq; aūt simul ñ duo s; un̄ ē x̄. ne sit
qrtas ñ trinitas ds̄. ac p h x̄ ē ds̄ aīa rāoīl 7 caro tanta ē ei unio utriq; nature. ut totū di-
cat̄ ds̄. totū hō 7 uicissim ds̄ hō. hō ds̄. qd̄ si dificile intelligit̄: mens fide p̄gēt. mag̃ magis-
q; ā peccātis abstinendo 7 bona opando. difficilia ei sc̄ h. Ut tn̄ h̄ic dicā: ñ aliud fuit illa di
sūm exinanitio: ñ forme seruil' .i. humane nature susceptio. Uerūq; g̃ ē in x̄ forma: qz utq; uia
7 plena ē in x̄ suba. In ɔūse ei 7 inalt̃abilit̃: unite sc̄ ad inuicē nature neq; diuina distante appa
simplicitate neq; humana aūt ɔūsa in ditatis naturam aūt in ñ existūtiā diuisa. neq; ex duab;
una fc̄a ē ɔposita natura. Xp̄c g̃ una p̄ ē geminę sube. ñ tn̄ ds̄ l' hō: pars huī p̄: dici p̄. Alioqn̄:
fili' di anq̄ susciperet formā serui: ñ erat tot'. 7 creuit cū hō diuinitati ei accessit. Sciendū tn̄
q̄ ñ semp fcm̄ ēē ad creationē refert̄ sic ibi. Dn̄e refugiū fc̄s es nob. Et itē fc̄s es m insalu-
tē. Non itaq; cāationis definitio l' edicio: h declarat̄. s; nob in refugiū l' in salutē ēē dr̄ qd̄
p' ñ erat. S; qrit p̄ cū nos saluatorē natū pfiteam: cū apl's fcm̄ eū dicat ex semine dd̄. cū
aliud sit fi. aliū nasci. q̄ 7 alio loco inqt. fcm̄ ē ex muliere. Aliq. g̃ significauit. h dicto. qz ei
ñ humano semine ēcreta. ē caro dn̄i in utō uirginis. 7 corp' effc̄a .s; effcū 7 uirtute sci sps:
id apl's dic̄ fcm̄ ñ natū. Aliud est semine admixto 7 sanginis coagulo generare: aliud ñ p
mixtione s; uirtute p creare. Possē hoīes gnāre filios hoīes .s; ñ face. Itē. Et si ñ incessit sem
hōis in ɔceptione uirginis: tn̄ qz ex ea carne x̄ formata ē q̄ ɔstat ex semine: recte dr̄ fc̄s ex
semine. Querens aūt utrū x̄ debeat dici cāta l' res creata simplicit̃: audiat augustinū sup
h ita differentē. In p̄ncipio erat ūbū 7 uerbū caro fcm̄ ē. pp̄ natiuitatē incarnationis ei
q̄ fc̄a ē in tpr̄ ex uirgine. 7 oīa p ipm̄ fc̄a sc̄. neq; dic̄ oīa. ñ q̄ fc̄a sc̄ .i. omnē creaturam. Un̄
liqdo apparet. ipm̄ fcm̄ ñ ēē p qm̄ fc̄a sc̄ oīa. Et si fc̄s ñ ē: cāta ñ ē. Si aūt creata ñ ē: eidem
cū pr̄e sube ē. Oīs ei suba q̄ ds̄ ñ ē: creata ē. 7 q̄ cāta ñ ē: ds̄ ē. S; si fili' ñ eidē sube ē cui'
pr̄: g̃ fc̄a suba ē. Et si fc̄a suba ē: ñ oīa p ipm̄ fc̄a sc̄. At omnia p ipm̄ fc̄a sc̄. fc̄a g̃ suba
ñ ē. Qui tn̄ sic ait apl's fc̄s ē ei .s. ad honorē pr̄is s̄ carnē. intellectus ū s̄ diuitate fc̄s dico: 7
spialit̃ ex semine dd̄. qz maria fuit de stirpe dd̄. ex cui' semine formata ē caro dn̄ica ope
spc̄ sci. in utō uirginali. S; attendendū ē qr spialit̃ h nominat dd̄. cū ɔstet: q. fc̄a ē pmissio
abrahe sicut 7 dd̄ .s; apl's uolens grām ɔm̄dare: maluit dicē de dd̄ q̄ 7 eminnos fuit: ñ
de semine abrahe q̄ iust' fuit. ut ñ p m̄ito s; grā nat' de eo puteē: 7 7 id: ut ex hōie rege
s carnē rex nat' ostendat̄. sic de dō rege: rex an sc̄la nat' ē deni ā uirtute ɔm̄dans eum
sub dd̄. Qui p̄destinat' ē fili' di in uirtute s spm̄ scificōnis ex resurrōne mortuoz ihu x̄
dn̄i nr̄i. h p̄mo uidendū ē qd̄ sit p̄destinatio. 7 de q̄ sit p̄dest. utrū de re q̄ semp fuit:
an de re q̄ ex tpr̄ fuit. 7 utr̄ de p̄ an de natura. 7 si de p̄ ē: p̄ea attendendū ē. s qm̄ natura
sit p̄destinata. Predestinatio ē: grē p̄patio q̄ ab eťno ds̄ hoī x̄ 7 cunctis q̄s p̄sciuit
ɔformes fi ymaginis filii sui: bona sua mitis p̄parauit. Preclarissimū ei lum̄ p̄de-
stinationis 7 grē: ē ip mediator di 7 hominū hō x̄ ihc. Ille ei hō ut a ūbo pat' coeťno
in unitatē p̄ assūpt' fili' di unigenit' eēt. un h m̄uit: q. ei' bonū q̄lecūq; p̄cessit. ut

Ae cōcilio toleta-
no .viii.
Au. in libro .iii.
d̄ trinitate d̄ in̄ car-
natoil. Nota 7 h
Au. sr̄ iohn.
Nota utrūq;.
Au. 7. iii. l. d̄ tri.
Au. d̄ fide ad petr̄.
Johs damasceni.
Ĉ illi' p̄ ñ sc̄ p̄ res
due nature.
Aug. i l'. d̄ trinita.
Aug. q̄re fcm̄ ñ
natū dicat apl's.
In libro ɔonū uet-
7 noui test'. q̄ ab
ignorantib; p̄titu
lat' dubitum.
Au. d̄ trinitate.
Au. x'. sup dicendo creata.
Au. i lib'. d̄ trin.
pp natiuitatē q̄
fc̄a ē ūbū dr̄ fcm̄.
Au. i eod.
Intende.
dimo.
dinb.
dinb.
Intende.
Au. in libro de
p̄destinatione
scōr. S.

Utille eni' hō
assūpt' a ūbo
unigenit' eēt.

Aug. in libro .iii. de trinitate. Fcm̄ qppe creaturam p quem facta est
omnis creatura. omnem creaturam teste habere oportebat.
Aug. in sermone de natiuitate domini. qui sic incipit.
Audistis fr̄s quemadmodū nob. O noua 7 inaudita ɔmixtio.
ō mira 7 iexquisita ɔpago. Ds̄ qui ē 7 q̄ erat cāator fit 7 creatura.

18. Stephen Langton, Commentary on Ruth: Oxford, Bodleian Library, MS Rawl. C. 427, fol. 66v.
s. xiii1/4: vicars choral of Hereford Cathedral.

Stephen Langton lectured on the entire Bible during his years in Paris between *c.* 1180 and 1206—the first scholar to do so since Rabanus Maurus. After a simple account of the *dramatis personae* (Ruth 1:1–2:1: fol. 66ra–rb), he turns to the allegorical content of his text: that Ruth 'is' the Gentile community that returned to Bethlehem (1:19) and found Christ (Boaz), while her sister-in-law Orpah 'is' the Jews, who turned back from Bethlehem and the field of Boaz. Langton mixes the established exegesis of Rabanus and the *Gloss* with unpredictable contemporary references and what may be *exempla* for preaching. 'The evangelists and the fathers have gathered the harvest; we modern masters glean what remains' (2:1: fol. 66vb; Lacombe, p. 98). The worm that dropped from Symeon Stylites's festering wound was caught by a pagan nobleman, in whose hand it turned to a precious jewel (1:20: fol. 66va).[1]

Parchment; i + 107 fol.; page 332 x 250 mm.; text 250 x 178 mm.; column 250 x 82/88 mm.; 50 lines per page. Pencil ruling, which varies from quire to quire; here 6 mm. boundary-columns frame the text. Biblical quotations are underlined in red—the same red that is used for chapter-numbers, paraph-signs and signs in the margin. The small regular script, which still uses the top line on the page, confirms a date in the first half of the century (Ker). The librarian who assembled the volume had fourteen quires,[2] all of the same dimensions but written by various scribes. Several of these are charter scribes, given to tall ascenders on the top line and unskilled in maintaining an even ductus through the page. The binding, the foliation on the verso of each quire (here lxvj), the red running heads in the upper margin and the marginal signs are all part of the librarian's original conception.

The volume as a whole consists of Langton's commentaries on I–IV Kings (fol. 1r–52v), on Judges and Ruth (fol. 53r–68v) and on the Minor Prophets (fol. 69r–106 + the fragmentary fol. 107r). The page shown here is Ruth 1:6–2:8. The marginalia on the right indicate M(oraliter) and N(ota), which recur in the text. Other pages indicate sources—Gregory the Great, Boethius, Rabanus, the *Gloss*—and turning-points in the text: 'argumentum', 'solutio'. Such 'sign-posts', which are characteristic of the Bible-commentaries of both Langton and Hugh of St. Cher (*ob.* 1263) may be literally the *postills* (? Old French 'postel') from which the later *Postillae* of Nicholas of Lyra are named. Here they indicate sources, structure and level of commentary, as Langton passes at will from the literal sense to the moral and the allegorical and back again.

Bibliography: G. Lacombe and B. Smalley, 'Studies on the Commentaries of Cardinal Stephen Langton', *Archives d'histoire doctrinale et littéraire du Môyen Age* 5 (1930) 5–220; N. R. Ker, 'From "Above Top Line" to "Below Top Line": A Change in Scribal Practice', *Celtica* 5 (1960) 13–16, rpt. in *Books, Collectors and Libraries: Studies in the Medieval Heritage,* ed. A. G. Watson (London, 1985), pp. 71–74; A. Saltman, *Stephen Langton, Commentary on the Book of Chronicles* (Ramat-Gan, 1978).

[1] Lacombe, p. 96; cf. *Vitae patrum I, Vita sancti Simeonis,* cap. 8 (*PL* 73:329).

[2] The quiring is: i–ii^{8}iii^{4}iv^{10}v^{8}vi^{4}vii^{10} (= I–IV Kings); viii^{6}ix^{10} (= Judges and Ruth); x–xiii^{8}xiv^{6} + a fragment (= Minor Prophets).

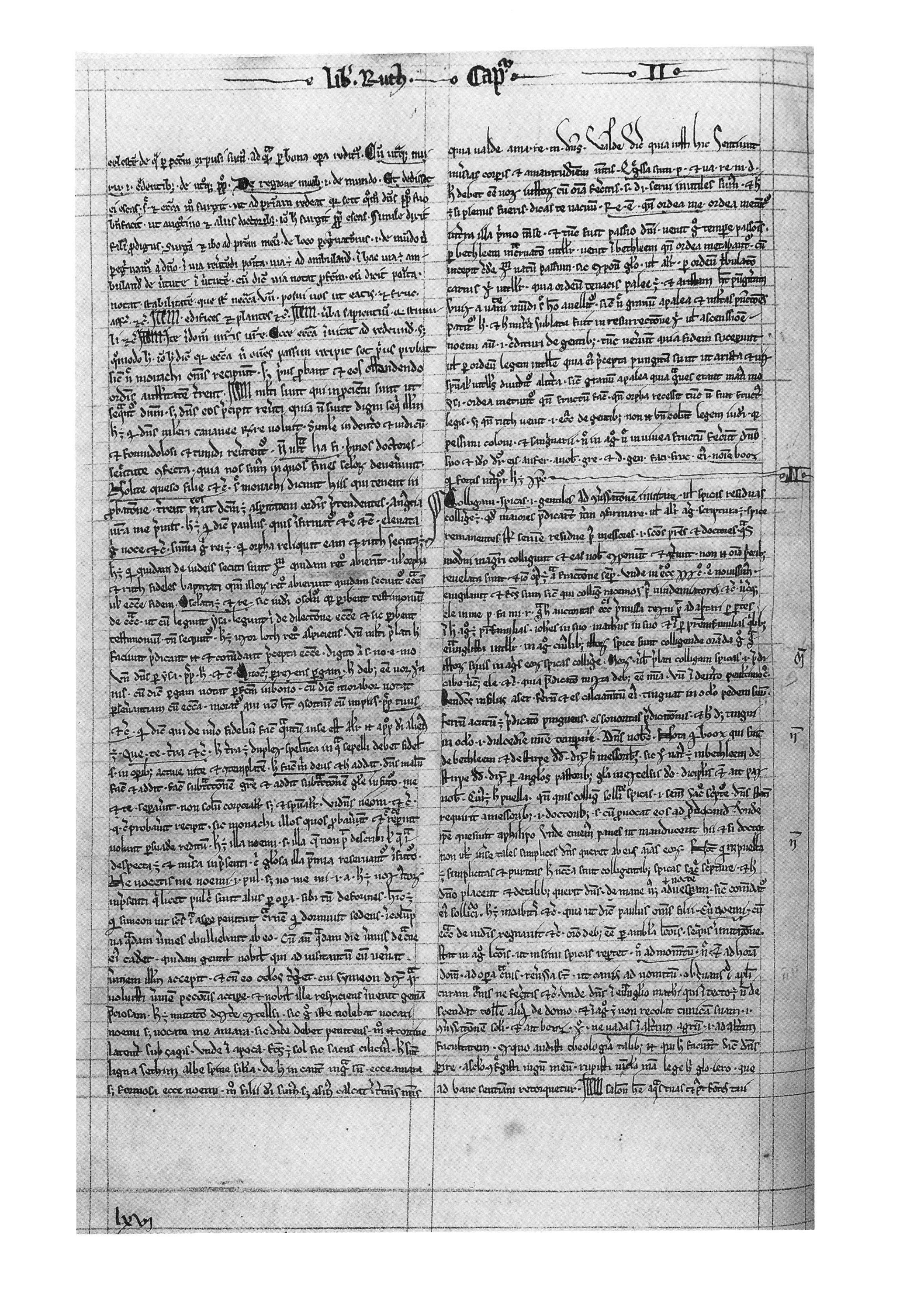

19. A 'Paris Bible': Princeton, N.J., William H. Scheide Library, Princeton University Library, MS 7, fol. 298v. s. xiii: ? Soissons.

A page of the Minor Prophets in a 'Paris Bible', showing the end of the prologue to Habakkuk and chapters 1–2:18. The Bible (fol. 1r–403rb) is followed, as often, by Jerome's glossary *De nominibus hebraicis* (fol. 404ra–439vb).

Parchment; iii + 439 + iii fol.; page 265 x 175 mm.; text 170 x 110 mm.; column 170 x 50 mm. Ruled with a pencil; upper margin 25 mm.; lower margin 70 mm. Foliation I-CCCCIII, 404–439. Binding s. xix, probably for Ashburnham.

French, mid-thirteenth century; erased armorial bearings (fol. 1: at the foot of both columns). The book is first recorded in the hands of Guglielmo Libri, dealer, forger and thief, who provided a false inscription (San Lorenzo el R[eal] del Escorial [fol. 1r]).[1] Libri sold it to the fourth earl of Ashburnham (*ob.* 1878) for his great collection in Sussex, whence it passed to another major collector, Henry Yates Thompson, and so via the London book trade to William Taylor Scheide in 1899.

The thin, flexible parchment, which enables this little book to run to almost 900 pages without being inconvenient to handle, is characteristic of these 'personal' Bibles of the thirteenth and fourteenth centuries. They were written by professional scribes, professionally illuminated, and acquired by private owners. The text is regarded by modern editors as broadly standard—'the Paris text' (Quentin)—but new corrections and new errors indicate that Paris Bibles were copied from various exemplars in various places; there was no centralized verification of the text, such as university masters endeavored to exercise over the transcription of their own academic lectures. In the present manuscript it is carefully divided into units of meaning by vertical hairlines that are just visible in the photograph, e.g. column 1, line 21, contra me/.

The *ad hoc* element in a 'Paris Bible' is vividly demonstrated in Robert Branner's analysis of the historiated initials in a small group of manuscripts, which includes Scheide 7 ('Soissons Bible', and *Manuscript Painting*, p. 216). All these manuscripts have artists in common, a number of the initials being signed in the margins with a distinctive mark or letter, on the same principle as a mason's mark. In Scheide 7 six initials are marked, very unobtrusively, θ: thus payment for that artist could be reckoned up when the manuscript was complete. But there is no correlation between an atelier of artists, who are jointly responsible for a group of manuscripts, and the textual traditions of these same manuscripts. Did the scholarly owner buy his manuscript and then specify the initials and/or artists in the atelier of his choice? Or did an atelier acquire miscellaneous, unembellished texts, illuminate them and offer them for public sale?

Bibliography: R. Branner, 'The "Soissons Bible" Paintshop in Thirteenth-Century Paris', *Speculum* 44 (1969) 13–34; *Manuscript Painting in Paris during the Reign of Saint Louis: A Study of Styles* (Berkeley, 1977); A. d'Esneval, 'La division de la Vulgate latine en chapitres dans l'édition parisienne du xiiie siècle, *Revue des sciences philosophiques et théologiques* 62 (1978) 559–68; Light, 'Versions' and 'The New Thirteenth-Century Bible and the Challenge of Heresy', *Viator* 18 (1987) 275–88; Petitmengin, 'Saint Louis'.

[1]As he did in the case of **no. 1**.

et reddet ei sapientissimus et clementissimus medicus. Sed o quo tempore debeam quod postulas dare. Non misereri, quia mira ista crudelitas et voluntas tua contra te petit. Ita et omnium noster sciens clementie sue pondera atque miserias interdum non exaudit clamantem, ut corripiatur et magis proficiat ad rogandum, et quasi igne excoctum iustiorem et puriorem faciat. Quod intelligens apostolus secundum id quod in iam est consecutus a domino ait: Sed non deficimus et sustinemus dominum in omni tempore. Et scit quia qui perseveraverit usque in finem hic salvus erit, et gloriatur in labore et dolore. Et ieremia dicit: Ut laborem et miseriam viderem. Ut quomodo alius invocat dominum sic iste vir et bellator invictus ad exercendum se et probandum tribulationem et miseriam venire desiderat. Incipit liber.

Onus quod vidit abachuc propheta. Usquequo domine clamabo et non exaudies? Vociferabor ad te vim patiens et non salvabis? Quare ostendisti mihi iniquitatem et laborem videre, predam et iniustitiam contra me? Quare respicis contemptores et taces conculcante impio iustiorem se? Et facies homines quasi pisces maris et quasi reptilia non habentia ducem; et factum est iudicium et contradictio potentior. Propter hoc lacerata est lex et non pervenit usque ad finem iudicium, quia impius prevalet adversus iustum; propterea egredietur iudicium perversum. Aspicite in gentibus et videte et admiramini et obstupescite, quia opus factum est in diebus vestris quod nemo credet cum narrabitur. Quia ecce ego suscitabo chaldeos gentem amaram et velocem ambulantem super latitudinem terre ut possideat tabernacula non sua. Horribilis et terribilis est; ex semetipsa iudicium et onus egredietur. Leviores pardis equi eius et velociores lupis vespertinis. Et diffundentur equites eius, equites namque eius de longe venient, volabunt quasi aquila festinans ad comedendum. Omnes ad predam venient; facies eorum ventus urens, et congregabit quasi harenam captivitatem. Et ipse de regibus triumphabit, et tyranni ridiculi eius erunt; ipse super omnem munitionem ridebit et comportabit aggerem et capiet eam. Tunc mutabitur spiritus et pertransibit et corruet; hec est fortitudo eius dei sui. Numquid non tu a principio domine deus meus sancte meus, et non moriemur. Domine in iudicium posuisti eum, et fortem ut corriperes fundasti eum. Mundi sunt oculi tui ne videas malum, et respicere ad iniquitatem non potes. Quare non respicis super iniqua agentes et taces impio devorante iustiorem se? Et facies homines quasi pisces maris et quasi reptile non habens principem. Totum in hamo sublevabit, traxit illud in sagena sua et congregavit in rete suo. Super hoc letabitur et exultabit. Propterea immolabit sagene sue et sacrificabit reti suo, quia in ipsis incrassata est pars eius et cibus eius electus. Propter hoc ergo expandit sagenam suam et semper interficere gentes non parcet.

II

Super custodiam meam stabo et figam gradum meum super munitionem, et contemplabor ut videam quid dicatur mihi et quid respondeam ad arguentem me. Et respondit mihi dominus et dixit: Scribe visum et explana eum super tabulas, ut percurrat qui legerit eum, quia adhuc visus procul et apparebit in finem et non mentietur. Si moram fecerit, expecta eum, quia veniens veniet et non tardabit. Ecce qui incredulus est non erit recta anima eius in semetipso. Iustus autem in sua fide vivet. Et quomodo vinum potantem decipit, sic erit superbus vir et non decorabitur, qui dilatavit quasi infernus animam suam, et ipse quasi mors et non adimpletur, et congregabit ad se omnes gentes et coacervabit ad se omnes populos. Numquid non omnes isti super eum parabolam sument et loquelam enigmatum eius, et dicetur: Ve ei qui multiplicat non sua; usquequo et aggravat contra se densum lutum? Numquid non repente consurgent qui mordeant te, et suscitabuntur lacerantes te, et eris in rapinam eis? Quia tu spoliasti gentes multas, spoliabunt te omnes qui reliqui fuerint de populis propter sanguinem hominis et iniquitatem terre civitatis et omnium habitantium in ea. Ve qui congregat avaritiam malam domui sue, ut sit in excelso nidus eius et liberari se putat de manu mali. Cogitasti confusionem domui tue; concidisti populos multos, et peccavit anima tua. Quia lapis de pariete clamabit, et lignum quod inter iuncturas edificiorum est respondebit. Ve qui edificat civitatem in sanguinibus et preparat urbem in iniquitate. Numquid non hec sunt a domino exercituum? Laborabunt enim populi in multo igni, et gentes in vacuum et deficient. Quia replebitur terra ut cognoscat gloriam domini quasi aque operientes mare. Ve qui potum dat amico suo mittens fel suum et inebrians ut aspiciat nuditatem eius. Repletus es ignominia pro gloria; bibe tu quoque et consopire. Circumdabit te calix dextere domini, et vomitus ignominie super gloriam tuam. Quia iniquitas libani operiet te, et vastitas animalium deterrebit eos de sanguinibus hominum et iniquitate terre et civitatis et omnium habitantium in ea. Quid prodest sculptile quia sculpsit illud fictor suus

20. A Hebrew-Latin Psalter: Leiden, Bibliotheek der Rijksuniversiteit, MS Scaliger Hebr. 8, fol. 5r.
s. xii$^{med.}$: English.

Scholars in the later twelfth century were at least as likely to understand a little Hebrew as they were to understand Greek: perhaps more likely, in that Hebrew was spoken in the Jewish communities in Mainz, Troyes, Paris and London, as Greek was not. But to read and write Hebrew was a rarer accomplishment, which it is perhaps surprising to see at all within Christian orthodoxy. Without a Hebrew-Latin grammar, the student's best hope was a bilingual version of a known text—rather as Bede may have improved his Greek from the Laudian Acts (**no. 2**). Scaliger Hebr. 8 is the oldest and one of the finest of such manuscripts to survive.

Parchment; 58 fol.; page 235 x 165 mm.; text 155 x 61 mm.; text + gloss 181 x 143 mm.; 29 lines. Ruled with a hard-point, with broad marginal panels to accommodate the gloss.

The Hebrew text shown here is Psalms 13:2–15:4. Although each line necessarily runs from right to left, the text as a whole is in the western order; i.e. the Hebrew text begins at the front of the book, not (as it should) at the back. It is the work of a Latin scribe, who lays out the Hebrew carefully and clearly, with the vowels marked throughout. The inner margin contains a line-by-line Latin translation; the outer margin has a substantial, and so far unidentified, spiritual commentary. Neither the translation nor the commentary runs to the end of the Psalter, though it was intended that they should do so, judging by the ruling. The illumination, which has an important role here in dividing one Psalm from the next, is entirely western in style. Eventually it may indicate where this book was made; at the moment all we know for certain is that John Sturrey, a monk of St. Augustine's, Canterbury, owned it in the fourteenth century.[1] Thereafter it passed from hand to illustrious hand: Humfrey, duke of Gloucester, Thomas More's son-in-law, and finally Joseph Scaliger in Leiden. In very broad terms we can say that it was written in England or northern France, but beyond that all is speculation.

Bibliography: M. Beit-Arié, *The Only Dated Hebrew Manuscript Written in England (1189CE) and the Problem of Pre-Expulsion Anglo-Hebrew Manuscripts* [Valmadonna Trust] (London, 1985) concerning Valmadonna Trust MS 1; G. I. Lieftinck, 'The *Psalterium Hebraycum* from St. Augustine's, Canterbury Rediscovered in the Scaliger Bequest at Leyden', *Transactions of the Cambridge Bibliographical Society,* 2.2 (1955) 97–104, pll. VI–VIII: R. Loewe, 'The Mediaeval Christian Hebraists of England: Herbert of Bosham and Earlier Scholars', *Transactions of the Jewish Historical Society of England* 17 (1951–52) 225–49; 'The Mediaeval Christian Hebraists of England: The *Superscriptio Lincolniensis*', *Hebrew Union College Annual* 28 (1957) 205–252; 'Latin *Superscriptio* Manuscripts of Portions of the Hebrew Bible Other than the Psalter', *Journal of Jewish Studies* 9 (1958), 63–71; B. Smalley, *Hebrew Scholarship among Christians in Thirteenth-Century England as Illustrated by Some Hebrew-Latin Psalters* [Society for Old Testament Studies] (Oxford, 1939).

[1] A. B. Emden, *Donors of Books to S. Augustine's Abbey Canterbury* (Oxford Bibliographical Society Occasional Publication, 4; Oxford, 1968), pp. 16–17.

משכיל דורש את אלהים: הכל סר
יחדו נאלחו אין עושה טוב אין גם
אחד: קבר פתוח גרונם לשונם
יחליקון חמת עכשוב תחת לשונם:
אשר פיהם אלה ומרמה מלא קלו
רגליהם לשפוך דם: מזל רם ופגע
רע בדרכיהם ודרך שלום לא ידעו
אין פחד אלהים לנגד עיניהם: הלא
ידעו כל פועלי און אכלי עמי אכלו
לחם יי לא קראו: שם פחדו פחד כי
אלהים בדור צדיק: עצת עני תבישו
כי יי מחסהו: מי יתן מציון ישועת
ישראל בשוב יי שבות עמו יגל
זמור יעקב ישמח ישראל:
לדוד A דני מי יגור באהלך
ומי ישכון בהר קדשך: הולך תמים
ופועל צדק ודובר אמת בלבבו: לא
רגל על לשונו לא עשה לרעהו רעה
וחרפה לא נשא על קרבו: נבזה בעיניו
נמאס את יראי יי יכבד נשבע להרע
ולא ימיר: כספו לא נתן בנשך ושוחד
על נקי לא לקח עושה אלה לא ימוט
לעולם: כתם לדוד
ש מרני אל כי חסיתי בך:
אמרת ליי אדני אתה טובתי בל עליך:
לקדושים אשר בארץ המה ואדירי
כל חפצי בם: ירבו עצבותם אחר
מהרו בל אסיך נסכיהם מדם ובל
אשא את שמותם על שפתי: אדני

F. THE NEW LITERACY

21. Bible historiale complétée: London, British Library, MS Royal 17.E.VII, vol. 1, fol. 9r. *a.* 1357: French.

The *Bible historiale complétée* is the fusion of two texts: the French version of the Bible, which was achieved in Paris *c.* 1235–60, and a French translation of Peter Comestor's *Historia scholastica.* The moving spirit was Guyart Des Moulins (1297), who lived and worked in the region of Amiens; but the definitive text seems to be Parisian, and its earliest manuscript 1314. From then on the *Bible historiale complétée* was widely and consistently current, often in high-quality manuscripts made for royal and aristocratic patrons. This was the Bible that the men and women who shaped lay culture expected to own.

Parchment; iv + 264 + iv fol.; page 398 x 285 mm.; tricolumnar text 260 x 183 mm.; column 260 x 55 mm.; 46 lines. Fine miniatures in grisaille, from the workshop of Jean Bondol (Meiss). This is the first (Genesis-Psalms) of a two-volume set. It is dated 12 January 1356/57 (1, fol. 230rc); the second volume (Proverbs-Apocalypse) confirms the year in an acrostic colophon (2, fol. 241r; see Watson).

In principle the *Bible historiale complétée* alternates between the 'straight' text of the Bible and the *Historia scholastica.* Thus the page shown here begins: 'enuesti (with "coats of skins") et dist. Or est Adam fait aussi comme li uns de nous sachant et bien et mal' (Gen. 3:22). The *Glose* and also the *Texte* give the implications of Adam's knowledge of good and evil: his expulsion from Paradise, lest he should eat also of the tree of life (Gen. 3:22–24). At the bottom of this first column comes 'Hystoire sur ceste partie deuant dicte, de Genesis'. This history is a translation of Peter Comestor (*PL* 198:1074D–75C). But the following *Glose*—why did God let man be tempted?—is new. The third column returns to the Bible proper ('selonc la Bible'), followed by Comestor on the same passage. In this way the alternating sections of the Bible and the *Historia scholastica* are further elaborated by *glose, texte* or (as often) *incidens.* Some of the material may already be found in thirteenth-century Latin manuscripts of the *Historia scholastica,* either as Latin glosses in the hand of the text scribe or marked off with a red line within a column of text.[1] But the greater part of this commentary is unknown both as to its author and as to whether it was first composed in Latin or in French.

By 1300 the serious reader wanted more than a plain text of Scripture. The cumulative perceptions of the Fathers and modern scholarship should be immediately at hand (clearly labeled) as a guide to each passage. In the twelfth century the best modern edition had been the *Glossa ordinaria,* in the fourteenth, for a wider public, it was the *Bible historiale complétée.* There the spirit was preserved of Peter Comestor's original preface:

> Opus aggredi me [socii] compulerunt, ad quod pro ueritate historiae consequenda recurrerent. . . . Porro a cosmographia Moysi inchoans, riuulum historicum deduxi, usque ad ascensionem Saluatoris, pelagus mysteriorum peritioribus relinquens. . . . De historiis quoque ethnicorum quaedam *incidentia* [my italics] pro ratione temporum inserui, instar riuuli, qui secus alueum diuerticula quae inuenerit replens praeterfluere tamen non cessat.

Bibliography: S. Berger, *La Bible française au Moyen Age* (Paris, 1884); G. Hasenohr, 'Bibles et psautiers' in *Mise en page,* pp. 317–27; R. P. McGerr, 'Guyart Desmoulins, the Vernacular Master of Histories, and His *Bible Historiale*', *Viator* 14 (1983) 21–44, with a useful appendix of texts; M. Meiss, *French Painting in the Time of Jean de Berry: The Late Fourteenth Century and the Patronage of the Duke,* 2 vols. (London, 1967) 1.20–23, 204; 2.375, 383–84; C. R. Sneddon, 'The "Bible du XIIIe siècle": Its Medieval Public in the Light of Its Manuscript Tradition' in W. Lourdaux and D. Verhelst, *The Bible and Medieval Culture* (Leuven, 1979), pp. 127–40; G. F. Warner and J. P. Gilson, *Catalogue of Western Manuscripts in the Old Royal and King's Collections,* 4 vols. (London, 1921) 2.260–61; Watson, *British Library,* no. 904 and pl. 238.

[1]The red demarcation line persists, e.g. in the Strassburg edition of *c.* 1474 (Hain *5529, Goff P-460), and some of the material survives as 'Additamenta' in *PL*198. The term *incidens* exactly describes this demarcated commentary that has been dropped into a column of text.

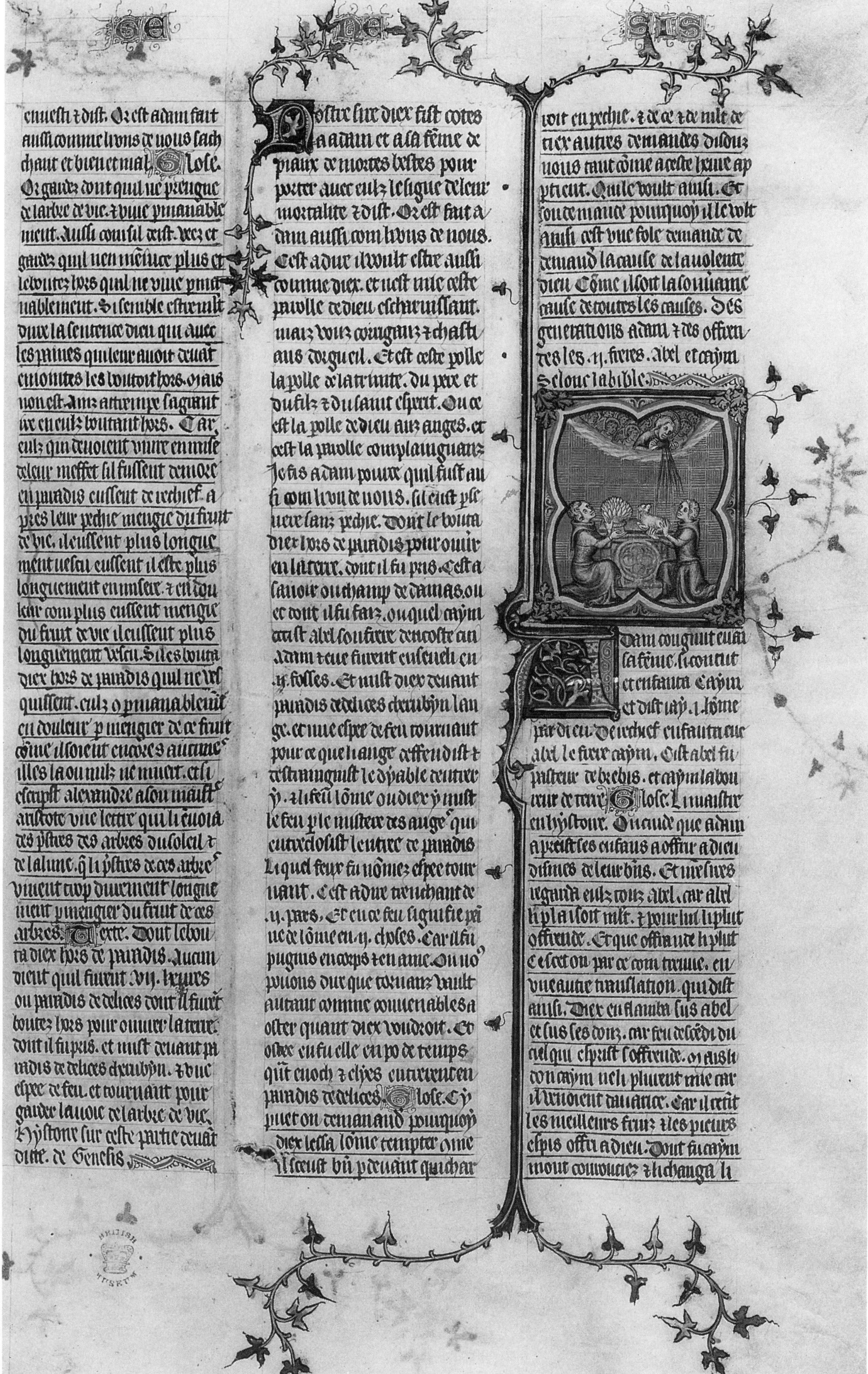
GE NE SIS

22. A Book of Hours: Notre Dame, Ind., University of Notre Dame, University Libraries, MS 4, fol. 135v–136r. s. xv3/4: Flemish, for the English market.

Christopher de Hamel has characterized Books of Hours as 'books for everybody', the one book that a family of moderate means would be likely to own. The manuscript shown here is a typical commercial production, made in Flanders (judging by the illumination) for the English market (judging by the Kalendar). It is a far cry from the *Très Riches Heures* of the Duc de Berry, or the Hours of Maximilian: a run-of-the-mill book that the respectable citizen or country gentleman could afford.

Parchment; v + 236 + v fol.; page 90 x 65 mm.; text 55 x 38 mm.; 17 lines. One scribe and one style of illumination throughout. Binding mid-seventeenth-century English. Twenty-eight full-page illuminations, all by the same artist and all on the verso of the page. The texts of the facing rectos have illuminated capitals and borders in the same muted style of blue, grey and brown, touched with gold. Careful quiring shows that the illuminated leaves (but not the rectos with text) are all singletons; that is, these pages were acquired by the stationer and dropped into their appropriate places when the scribe had finished his work.

Psalm 6, 'Domine ne in furore tuo arguas me', is the first of the Penitential Psalms. Having engineered the death of Uriah the Hittite, husband of Bathsheba, King David seeks forgiveness. Here Bathsheba is present only by implication. Some late Books of Hours take another angle on the story, showing the temptation to which David had succumbed—Bathsheba naked as she went down with her ladies to bathe. But the episode itself is standard, that of the repentant king. What is relatively unusual is that the Hours of the Virgin (fol. 49v–105r) are illustrated not with scenes relating to the Virgin (the Annunciation, Nativity, etc.), but with scenes from the Passion of Christ.

The coat of arms inside the front cover is that of the Regency country gentleman and bibliophile, Robert Bidulph Phillipps, of Longworth, Herefordshire, whose collection passed in 1864 to Belmont Abbey (Hereford).[1]

Bibliography: J. A. Corbett, *Catalogue of the Medieval and Renaissance Manuscripts of the University of Notre Dame* (Notre Dame, Ind., 1978), pp. 32–47; 'A Fifteenth-Century Book of Hours of Salisbury', *Ephemerides liturgicae* 71 (1957) 293–307, with two illustrations (fol. 34v–35r and 87v–88r); C. de Hamel, *A History of Illuminated Manuscripts* (Oxford, 1986), chap. 6 and pp. 248–49; G. Hasenohr, 'L'essor des bibliothèques privées aux XIVe et XVe siècles' in Vernet, pp. 214–63; V. Leroquais, *Les livres d'heures manuscrits de la Bibliothèque nationale,* 3 vols. and supplt. (Paris, 1927 and 1943); R. S. Wieck, *Time Sanctified: The Book of Hours in Medieval Art and Life* (New York, 1988).

[1] J. Burke, *A Genealogical and Heraldic History of the Commoners of Great Britain and Ireland* (London, 1833–38) 4.163–64; A. N. L. Munby, *Phillipps Studies* (Cambridge, 1951–60), 5.115. He belonged to the circle of Sir Thomas Phillipps, the monomaniacal collector.

Incipiunt septem psalmi
antiphona Ne reminiscaris.
Domine ne
in furore tu
o arguas
me neque in
ira tua cor
ripias me. Miserere me
i domine quoniam infirmus sum
sana me domine quoniam con
turbata sunt omnia ossa
mea. Et anima mea tur
bata est valde sed tu domi
ne usquequo. Convertere
domine et eripe animam me
am salvum me fac pro
pter misericordiam tuam. Quoniam

non est in morte qui memor
sit tui in inferno autem quis
confitebitur tibi. Labo
ravi in gemitu meo lava
bo per singulas noctes lec
tum meum lacrimis me
is stratum meum rigabo.
Turbatus est a furore o
culus meus inveteravi i
nter omnes inimicos me
os. Discedite a me omnes
qui operamini iniquita
tem. quoniam exaudivit dominus
vocem fletus mei. Exau
divit dominus deprecationem
meam dominus orationem
meam suscepit. Erubes

cant et conturbentur vehe
menter omnes inimici mei;
convertantur et erubescant
valde velociter. Gloria.
Beati quorum remisse
sunt iniquitates et
quorum tecta sunt peccata.
Beatus vir cui non impu
tavit dominus peccatum nec est
in spiritu eius dolus. Quoniam
tacui inveteraverunt ossa
mea dum clamarem tota
die. Quoniam die ac noc
te gravata est super me ma
nus tua conversus sum
in erumpna mea dum con
figitur spina. Delictum

23. The Wycliffite Bible: Oxford, Christ Church, MS 145, fol. 232r. *c.* 1400: English.

> A symple creature hath translatid the Bible out of Latyn into English. First this symple creature hadde myche trauaile with diuerse felawis and helperis to gedere manie elde biblis, and othere doctouris and comune glosis, and to make oo [one] Latyn bible sumdel trewe; and thanne to studie it of the newe, the text with the glose, and othere doctouris as he michte gete, and speciali Lire on the elde testament that helpide ful myche in this werk. The thride tyme to counseile with elde gramariens and elde dyuynis of harde wordis and harde sentencis, hou tho michten best be vndurstonden and translatid. The fourthe tyme to translate as cleerli as he coude to the sentence, and to haue manie gode felawis and kunnynge at the correcting of the translacioun.

This 'honest translator' sounds like a university man, writing for an academic audience.[1] That appears to be the context in which the Wycliffite Bible, the first complete English version of the Vulgate, originated. Although Wyclif was neither the author nor demonstrably the patron, he created the climate in which Oxford clerics wanted to have the Bible in English, even though they themselves could easily read it in Latin.

Parchment; iii + 386 fol.; page 388 x 265 mm.; text 262 x 182 mm.; column 262 x 85 mm.; 58 lines. The script is a good plain *textualis,* the initials blue with flourishing in red. The running heads and chapter-numbers are also in alternating red and blue. The opening initial to Jerome's prologue, 'Brother Ambrose' (*Frater Ambrosius:* fol. 10r) has a gold background and a half-border round the page. This splendid one-volume Bible is in its original binding of tawed leather on wood with two clasps (missing)—an English pandect. The earliest provenance is the Saunders family in Northamptonshire in 1575 (fol. 1r).

The page shown is Isaiah 53:1–10 in the 'early version', which follows the Vulgate as closely as possible in both vocabulary and syntax (Hudson, 1978, p. 40). Even so, the itch to improve led to further revisions and critical annotation. MS Bodley 959 is a working text of the 'early version' which shows the translator occasionally shifting ground towards normal English speech. The authors of the 'late version' (to which most of the 250 surviving manuscripts belong) were readier to accept this principle, but still cautious (Hudson 1978, *ad loc.*). Thus in the broader context of European vernacular translation the Wycliffite Bible is within the tradition of literal translation found in the Paris Bible of *c.* 1250 and the mid-fourteenth-century German translation that was printed by Mentelin a century later (1466, see **no. 28**). There is no English equivalent of the *Bible historiale complétée* (**no. 21**) or the *Klosterneuburger Evangelienbuch* (*c.* 1330: Kornrumpf in Reinitzer, *Vestigia*).

In contrast to the run of translations in the late fourteenth century, in which a patron would commission his own English version of a favorite book,[2] translating the Bible was an ongoing academic task. Like the radical critics of the contemporary Church, it probably had its beginnings in a few Oxford colleges, notably Queen's. As these critics fed into the wider movement of Lollardy, so the Wycliffite Bible is found in dissenting circles throughout the fifteenth century. It never saw print.[3] Mentelin's German Vulgate has no counterpart in England. Thus the English Bible, when it does come, is a fresh start from the editions and translations of the sixteenth century.

Bibliography: C. Lindberg, *MS Bodley 959: Genesis-Baruch 3:20 in the Earlier Version of the Wycliffite Bible,* 5 vols. (Stockholm Studies in English, 6, 8 10, 13, 20; Stockholm, 1959–69), here 20.154. A. Hudson, *Selections from English Wycliffite Writings* (Cambridge, 1978), nos. 6 and 14; *The Premature Reformation* (Oxford, 1988); H. Reinitzer, *Deutsche Bibelübersetzungen des Mittelalters* (Vestigia Bibliae, 9–10, for 1987–88; Bern, 1991).

---

[1]This preface is later than both the early and late versions of the Wycliffite Bible itself; the author cannot be reliably identified. See further A. Hudson, 'John Purvey: A Reconsideration of the Evidence for His Life and Writings', *Viator* 12 (1981) 355–80, at pp. 374–77.

[2]See for example R. Hanna, 'Sir Thomas Berkeley and His Patronage', *Speculum* 64 (1989) 878–916, with reference to Trevisa.

[3]See p. 13 above.

to me my puple & my kinrage me here þe. for lawe
fro me shal gon out. & my dom in to li3t of puplis shal
resten. Ne3 is my ri3twise. gon out is my saueour.
& myn armys puplis shul deme. me ylis shuln abi
de. & myn arm susteneu. rereþ in to heuene 3oure
e3en & seeþ vnder erþe bynepen. for heuenes as smoke
shal melten & þe erþe as a cloþ shal be totreden. & his
dwellers as þese shul dien. myn helþe forsoþe in to euer
more shal ben. & my ri3twisnesse shal not failen. he
reþ me þat knowen þe ri3twise. 3ee puple my lawe
in þe herte of hem. Wileþ not dreden reprof of men. & þe
blasfemes of hem dredeþ not. As forsoþe cloþing so
shal ete hem a werm. & as wlle so shal deuouren hem
þe mo3te. myn helþe forsoþe in to euermore shal ben.
& my ri3twisnesse in to generaciouns & generaciouns. rys rys
cloþe þou strengþe þe arm of þe lord. rys as in þe olde da
3is in generaciouns of worldis. Wheþer not þou smyte þe proude.
woundedist þe dragoun. wheþer not þou driedist þe se. þe water
of þe huge depþe. þe whiche puttist þe depþe of þe
se weie. þat gon on shulden than diliuered. & now þat ben
a3een bo3t of þe lord shul turnen a3een & comen in to sion
preisende. & euerlastende gladnesse on þe hedis of hem.
Ioye & gladnesse þei shuln holden. flee shal sorewen
& weiling. lo I þeself shal comforten 3ou. Who þou þat
þou drede of a deadli man. & of þe sone of man þat as
hei so shal ware dreie. & hast for3eten þe lord þi makere
þat beinte heuenes & foundide þe erþe. & inreddist
contynuelli al dai fro þe face of his wodnesse þat hee
troblede. & hadde ordeyned to lesen. Where is now
þe wodnesse of þe trouble. Sone shal comen þe goere
to openen & shal not slen vnto þe werre slau3t. ne fai
len shal his bred. I forsoþe am þe lord þi god þat
disturbe þe se. & swellen his flodis. þe lord of ostis my
name. I sette my wordis in þi mouþ & in þe shadewe
of myn hond I defendede þee. þat þou plaunte heuenes
& founde erþe. & seie to sion my puple þou art. be reisid
be reised rys þou ierusalem. for þou dronke of þe hond of þe
lord þe chalis of his wraþe. vnto þe grounde of þe
chalys of slep þou dronke. & þou drunke it vp vnto þe drestis.
þer is not þat susteine hir of alle þe sones þat she gat. &
of þer is not þat take hir hond alle þe sones þat she nurshi
de vp. Two þingis ben þat a3en camen to þee. Who
shal sorewen vpon þee. wastite & tobrising. & hunger
& swerd. Who shal comforte þee. þe sones ben ouer
cast. þei slepten in þe hed of alle weies. as þe vnicor
ne beste grened þat is clepid orix. ful of þe indig
nacioun of þe lord blamyng of þi god. þerfore here þou
þese þingis þou porelet & drunken. not of wyn. þese
þingis seiþ þe lordshipere þi lord & þi god þat fau3t
for his puple. lo I toc of þin hond þe chalis of sleep.
þe grounde of þe chalis of myn indignacioun. I shal not
leyn to þat þou drinke it more. & I shal poten it in þe
hond of hem þat þee mekeden. & seiden to þi soule.
be þou bowid in þat wee passe. and þou puttist as erþe
þi bodi & as a weie to goeres. LII.
Ris rys be þou clad þou sion wiþ þi strengþe. be þou clad wiþ
þe cloþis of þi glorie þou ierusalem cite of þe holi. for he shal
not lenger more þat þou passe bi þee an vncircumcidid & vncle
ne. Be þou shaken out of þe poudre. rys sit þou ierusalem. loose
þe boundis of þi necke þou caitif dou3ter of sion. for þese
þingis seiþ þe lord. freeli 3ee ben sold. & wiþouten
siluer 3ee shul ben a3een bo3t. for þese þingis seiþ þe lord
god. In to egipt cam doun my puple in þe bigynnyng.
as a comeling where he was þere. & assur wiþoute
eny cause chalengede hym. & now what to me is þis
seiþ þe lord. for taken awei is my puple wiþoute cau
se. his lordshiperes wickeli diden seiþ þe lord. & by
sili al dai my name is blasfemyd. for þat witen shal
my puple my name in þat dai. for I þeself þat spac
lo I am nee3. hou faire vp on mounteynes þe feet of
þe tellende & prechende pees. tellende good. prechende hel
the seiende. sion regne shal þi god. þe vois of þi wo
tes. þei reiseden a vois. togidre þei shul preisen. for wiþ
e3e to e3e þei shul seen. whanne conuerten shal þe lord sion.
Ioyeþ & preiseþ togidre 3ee desertis of ierusalem. for comfortid
haþ þe lord his puple. a3een bo3t he haþ ierusalem. redy
made þe lord his holi arm in þe e3en of alle ientils.
& seen shuln alle cuntreis of erþe þe helþe 3iuere of oure
god. Goþ awey goþ awey goþ out þenus. þe defoulid
þing wileþ not touchen. goþ out fro þe myddel
of it. Be 3ee clensid þat bern þe vessels of þe lord.
for not in noise 3ee shul gon out ne in fli3t 3ee shul
gon forþ. forsoþe gon biforn 3ou shal þe lord. & gedre
togidre 3ou shal þe god of israel. lo vnderstonde shal my
seruaunt. & ben enhauncid & reisid. & ful hei3 he shal
be gretly. As stoneieden on hym manye. so vnglori
ous shal ben among men his si3te. & þe fourme of hym
among þe sones of men. he shal springe manye ientils.
vp on hym togidre holden shul kingis þer mouþ. for to whom
is not told of hym shul see. & þat herden not biheelden. LIII.
Lord who leeuede to oure heering. & þe arm
of þe lord to whom is it shewid. & it shal
stezen vp as a quik heg biforn hym. & as a ro
te fro þe pristende erþe. þer is not shap to hym ne
fairnesse. & wee se3en hym & he was not of si3te. and
wee desireden hym dispisid & þe last of men man of
sorewis & witende infirmyte. & as hid is his che
re & dispisid. wherfore ne wee setten bi hym. Verreli ou
re sykenesses he toc. & oure sorewis he bar. & wee
heelden hym as leprous & smyten of god & meekid.
he forsoþe woundid is for oure wickidnesses. defou
lid is for oure hidous giltis. þe disciplyne of oure
pes on hym. & wiþ his wannesse wee ben helid. alle
wee as sheep erreden. eche in to his weie bowede
doun. & þe lord putte in hym þe wickidnesse of vs
alle. he is offrid for he wolde. & he openede not
his mouþ. as a sheep to sleyng he shal be lad. &
as a lomb biforn þe clippere itself. he shal bicome
doumb. & he openede not his mouþ. fro anguish & fro
dom he is taken awey. þe generacioun of hym who shal
tellen out. for kut awei he is fro þe lond of lyueres.
for þe hidous gilte of my puple I smot hym. & 3iuen
he shal vnpitouse men for biriyng. & riche men
for his deþ for þi þat wickidnesse he dide not. ne
trecherie was in his mouþ. & þe lord wolde to
treden hym in infirmyte. If he shul poten hys

24. Fifth Edition of the Block-book Apocalypse: Oxford, Bodleian Library, Auct. M.III.15, p. 21. *c.* 1465–70: German.

The text of Apocalypse 12:13–14 is given in full: in the upper picture (12:14) 'Date sunt mulieri due ale aquile magne ut volaret in desertum locum ubi alitur per tempus et tempora et dimidium tempus [sic] a facie serpentis' and in the lower picture (12:13) 'Postquam uidit draco quod proiectus fuisset in terra persecutus est mulierem que peperit masculum'. The final sentence, that 'Mother Church has passed through the wilderness' expresses an allegory familiar from the time of Bede (*PL* 93:168B).

Technically the block-book is a series of wood-cuts with text and picture engraved together; the sequence as a whole is ordered by large capital letters, here L. Paper; 48 fol.; page 251 x 195 mm.; hand-colored crimson, red, yellow, green, black. Auct. M.III.15 (like some other copies of the fifth edition) has an extensive German commentary interleaved throughout (Palmer).

In the block-book Apocalypse the Bible text is set within the life of St. John the Divine. The opening scenes show him preaching, baptizing a convert and being sent to the emperor Domitian, who exiles him to Patmos. At the end he says his last Mass, his body lies in the tomb but his soul is carried aloft by an angel. The reader is thus encouraged to identify with St. John and follow him into the other world (Klein). In this convention and in other iconographic and textual details the block-book Apocalypse belongs to the tradition of illustrated Apocalypses that are such a marked feature of English and French illumination from the mid-thirteenth century to the early fourteenth (Bing, Morgan). Even the *mise-en-page* follows one of the two established traditions: compare Oxford, Bodleian Library, MS Auct. D.IV.17 [Coxe] and contrast MS Douce 180 [Klein].

What is harder to understand is how and by whom these block-books were used. The crudity of the execution suggests a popular audience, that those are *Volksbücher* (Schmitt, in *Blockbücher,* pp. 215–20). But why then is the text in Latin? Within the technology of the day (1460+), they are not really books; yet the appearance of six editions (Kristeller) within twenty years indicates a ready market. But still it was relatively a luxury market: institutional libraries and the substantial bourgeoisie, literate in both Latin and German (Schneider, in *Blockbücher,* pp. 35–57). A clue to their social level is the note (fol. 2): 'Bittend got für den armen sunder geber diess buchss uwer bruder diether von Hentschussheym'. Dieter's family name persists in the Handschuhsheim suburb of present-day Heidelberg (Palmer). Such owners were far from radical. The block-book Apocalypse offers within its pictures no textual or visual innovation; rather it presents the *via regia* of the Vulgate text with its traditional, accredited commentary.

Bibliography: H. O. Coxe, *The Apocalypse of St. John the Divine . . . from a MS. [Auct. D.IV.17] in the Bodleian Library* (Roxburghe Club; London, 1876); P. K. Klein, *Apocalypse: MS. Douce 180* (Codices selecti, 72; Graz, 1983); E. Purpus, *Die Apokalypse Blockbuch-Ausgabe IVE: Mainz, Gutenberg-Museum, Ink. 131* (Monumenta xylographica et typographica, 1; Munich, 1991), with color microfiches. G. Bing, 'The Apocalypse Block-Books and Their Manuscript Models', *Journal of the Warburg Institute* 5 (1942) 143–58; *Blockbücher des Mittelalters: Bilderfolgen als Lektüre (Gutenberg-Museum, Mainz, 22 Juni–1 September 1991)* (Mainz, 1991); P. Kristeller, *Die Apokalypse: Älteste Blockbuchausgabe in Lichtdrucknachbildung* (Berlin, 1916), an overview of editions one to six (here no. 44, p. 38); N. Morgan, *The Lambeth Apocalypse* (London, 1990); N. F. Palmer, 'Latein und Deutsch in den Blockbüchern' in *Latein und Volkssprache im deutschen Mittelalter: 1100–1500,* ed. N. Henkel and N. F. Palmer (Tübingen, 1992), pp. 310–36; W. L. Schreiber, *Manuel de l'amateur de la gravure sur bois et sur métal au XVe siècle,* 8 vols. (Berlin, 1891–1911). Schreiber vols. 7–8 gives an overview of all the texts printed as block-books. Characteristic subjects are the *Biblia pauperum,* Antichrist and the Fifteen Signs of Judgment, the Lord's Prayer, the Marvels of the City of Rome, the Dance of Death and (twelve editions) the *Ars moriendi.* The essential update is *Blockbücher,* pp. 354–412.

Date sunt mulieri due ale aquile magne ut volaret in desertũ locũ ubi alitur ꝑ tempus et tempa et dimidiũ temp9 a facie serpentis
Postquã vidit draco q ꝓiectus fuisset in terram ꝑsecutus est mulierem que pepit masculum
Mater ecclesia trasiuit in heremo

G. THE BIBLE IN PRINT

25. The 'Editio princeps' of the Vulgate, Mainz 1453/55 (Johannes Gutenberg): Oxford, Bodleian Library, Arch. B.b.11, vol. II (not foliated).

The Gutenberg Bible is a two-volume folio for institutional use: in church or as a lectern Bible for reading in chapter or *ad collationem*. Of a print-run of between 150 and 200 copies, 48 are wholly or substantially extant, not counting fragments (Needham). So high a survival-rate is remarkable in a book that was textually and technically superseded within fifty years.

Paper; 319 fol.; page 402 x 288 mm.; text 287 x 195 mm.; column 287 x 86 mm.; fol. 1r–5r, 40 lines, fol. 5v, 41 lines, fol. 6r onwards 42 lines. This volume contains Proverbs–Apocalypse, *expl.* fol. 317v; charts of biblical history based on Peter of Poitiers have been added by hand to fol. 318r–19v. Remnants of the original binding have a fifteenth-century donation-note by 'Erhardus Neninger magister ciuium [sc. Bürgermeister] in Heylsprum' to the Carmelite house in Heilbronn-am-Neckar (dioc. Würzburg). The volume was rebound in Paris 1785 and acquired by the Bodleian in 1793 at the give-away price of £100 (Macray, p. 275).

Neither the text nor the layout of the Gutenberg Bible is yet fully understood in its later medieval context. In Quentin's Vulgate it has the siglum 'a', and in broad terms keeps company with the Paris text of the thirteenth century. H. Schneider argued for later local manuscripts, without really making his case. More recently the layout has been usefully compared with the Dominican refectory Bibles, the pattern of which was established at S. Jacques in the 1230s (König, 1979). The decoration in such Bibles is strictly practical: initials in diminishing size for books, chapters and Psalter-verses, but no full-page miniatures or elaborate borders. So in the Gutenberg Bible the text is disposed to accommodate rubrication and initials that will guide the reader; further illumination (if any) would be provided not in the workshops of Mainz but by an owner or patron according to his own taste.[1]

Gutenberg's command of text and technology was not equaled by either his own commercial sense or the security available for this new aspect of the book trade in the Middle Rhine. He had to invest heavily in machinery and materials and wait for his return. By comparison with the contemporary Flemish trade in Books of Hours,[2] Gutenberg's enterprise was speculative to a degree and dangerously underfinanced.

Bibliography: Hain *3031; BMC 1.17; Goff B-526; GW 4201; Proctor *56. S. Corsten and R. W. Fuchs, *Der Buchdruck im 15. Jahrhundert I: Bibliographie* (Stuttgart, 1988), pp. 281–307; H. Hummel, *Katalog der Incunabeln des Stadtarchivs Heilbronn* (Heilbronn, 1981); E. König, 'Die Illuminierung der Gutenbergbibel' in Schmidt and Schmidt-Künsemüller (below), pp. 69–125; 'The Influence of the Invention of Printing on the Development of German Illumination' in *Manuscripts in the Fifty Years after the Invention of Printing*, ed. J. B. Trapp (London, 1983), pp. 85-94; W. D. Macray, *Annals of the Bodleian Library*, 2nd ed. (Oxford, 1890; rpt. Oxford, 1984); P. Needham, 'The Paper Supply of the Gutenberg Bible', *Papers of the Bibliographical Society of America* 79 (1985) 303–374; G. Powitz, *Die Frankfurter Gutenberg-Bibel: Ein Beitrag zum Buchwesen des 15 Jahrhunderts* (Frankfurter Bibliotheksschriften, 3; Frankfurt-am-Main, 1990); W. Schmidt and F. A. Schmidt-Künsemüller, *Johannes Gutenbergs Zweiundvierzigzeilige Bibel: Kommentarband* (Munich, 1979); C. Schneider, 'Gutenberg—der Erfinder und seine Bücher' in *Gutenberg: 500 Jahre Buchdruck in Europa* (Ausstellungskataloge der Herzog August Bibliothek Wolfenbüttel; Wolfenbüttel, 1990), pp. 45–52; H. Schneider, *Der Text der Gutenbergbibel zu ihrem 500 jährigen Jubiläum untersucht* (Bonner biblische Beiträge; Bonn, 1954).

[1] König, 1979 and 1983.

[2] C. de Hamel, *A History of Illuminated Manuscripts* (Oxford, 1986), p. 183 *et passim.*

Lucas sirus · natõe anthi-
ocensis · arte medic⁹ · disci-
pulus apostoloꝝ · postea
paulū secut⁹ usq; ad con-
fessionē ei⁹ serviens dño sine crimine:
nam neq; uxorem unq̃ habuit neq; filios: septuaginta et quatuor annorū
obijt in bithinia · plen⁹ spiritu sancto.
Qui cū iam scripta essent euāgelia · p
matheū quidē in iudea · p marcū aūt
in italia: sancto instigante spiritu in
achaie partibz hoc scripsit euangeliū:
significans etiā ipē in principio ante
suū alia esse descripta. Cui extra ea q̃
ordo euāgelice dispositionis exposcit-
ta maxime necessitas laboris fuit: ut
primū grecis fidelibz omni ꝓphetati-
one venturi in carnē dei cristi manife-
stata humanitate ne iudaicis fabulis
attenti: in solo legis desiderio tenerē-
tur: uel ne hereticis fabulis et stultis
solicitationibz seducti exciderent a veritate elaboraret: dehinc · ut in principio euangelij iohānis natiuitate pre-
sumpta · cui euangelium scriberet et in
quo elect⁹ scriberet indicaret: cõtestās i
se cõpleta esse · q̃ essent ab alijs incho-
ta. Cui ideo post baptismū filij dei a
pfectione generatõnis ī cristo implete ·
repetende a pricipio natiuitatis humane potestas pmissa ē: ut requirentibz
demonstraret in quo apprehendēs e-
rat per nathan filiū dauid introitu re-
currentis ī deū generationis admisso ·
indisparabilis dei pdicās in hominibus cristū suū · pfecti opus hoīs redire
in se p filiū faceret: qui per dauid patrē
uenientibus iter pbebat in cristo. Cui
luce non immerito etiā scribēdorum
actuū apostoloꝝ potestas ī ministerio
datur: ut deo in deū pleno et filio pdi-
tionis extincto · oratone ab apostolis
facta · sorte domini electionis numer⁹
compleretur: sicq; paulus cõsumma-
tionē apostolicis actibz daret · quē diu
cõtra stimulū recalcitrantē dñs elegis-
set. Quod et legentibz ac requirentibz
deū · et si per singula expediri a nobis
utile fuerat: sciens tamē q operātem
agricolā oporteat de suis fructibus e-
dere · vitauim⁹ publicā curiositatem:
ne nō tā volentibz deū demõstrare vide-
remur · quā fastidientibus prodidisse.

Explicit pfacio. Incipit euangelium
secundum lucam · Prohemium ipsius beati luce in euangelium suum.

Quoniā quidē multi co-
nati sūt ordinare nar-
ratões q̃ ī nobis com-
plete sūt reꝝ · sicut tradi
derūt nobis q̃ ab initio
ipsi viderūt · et ministri
fuerūt sermonis: visū ē et michi assecuto
omīa a pricipio diligēter ex ordīe tibi
scribere optīe theophile: ut cognoscas
eoꝝ verboꝝ de qbz erudit⁹ es veritatē.

Fuit in diebus herodis regis iudee sacerdos quidam
nomine zacharias de vi-
ce abia · et uxor illi de filiabus aaron: et nomen eius elizabeth.
Erant autem iusti ambo ante deum:
incedentes in omnibus mandatis et
iustificationibus domini sine quere-
la. Et non erat illis filius · eo q esset elizabeth sterilis: et ambo processissent ī diebz suis. Factū est aūt cū sacerdotio fungeretur zacharias in ordine vicis sue ante deū: sedm cõsuetudi-
nem sacerdotij sorte exijt ut incensum
poneret ingressus in templū domini.
Et omīs multitudo ppli erat orās foris hora incensi. Apparuit autem illi
angelus dñi: stans a dextris altaris

26. Erasmus's Translation of Luke and John: London, British Library, MS Royal 1.E.V, vol. 1, fol. 205v. 7 September 1509 and 1522+: John Colet.

The second in a series of fair copies of Erasmus's translation of the New Testament: written by Peter Meghen, the one-eyed German scribe who was often employed by Erasmus himself, but not exclusively by him (Trapp, 1975). Here Meghen transcribed the Vulgate text for Colet (1509) and Erasmus's translation for an unknown patron a few years after Colet's death.

Paper; iii + 311 + ii fol.; page 450 x 295 mm.; text 315 x 183 mm.; 12 lines. Full-page author-portraits of Luke (fol. 3r) and John (fol. 171r) by a Flemish illuminator of the school of Simon Bening of Bruges (Dogaer, pp. 171–77).

The main text is the Vulgate, with the name of Jesus in gold, dominical words in red and citations of other passages of Scripture (none on this page) in blue. Erasmus's translation from the Greek is set at half-spacing in the outer margin. In the page shown here (John 6:32–34) he proposes for instance the more specific and emphatic '*illum* panem' (lines 3–4) and 'panis enim *dei*' (line 8), and the radically different 'non sitiet *unquam*', as against 'in eternum' (lines 23–24). Erasmus justified his divergence from the text in common use on three criteria: the Greek original, patristic quotation of the Latin Bible, and his own restoration of corrupt readings. His *Novum instrumentum* (1516), the Greek New Testament with the Vulgate in parallel, has an appendix of *Annotationes,* which was increased with each subsequent edition (Reeve). Here 'in eternum' (John 6:34) was eventually justified:

> Graecis est πώποτε, id est, Vnquam, Atque itidem habet codex aureus.[1]

In the second edition of the *Novum instrumentum* (1519) the Vulgate is replaced with Erasmus's own translation from the Greek: the *Annotationes* now follow the version to which they properly refer. In the three editions following (1522, 1527 and 1535) these notes are further revised and amplified. Thus the present manuscript spans over a decade of philological research in the cause of a reliable Latin New Testament.

Bibliography: H. Gibaud, *Un inédit d'Erasme: la première version du Nouveau Testament* (Angers, 1982). J. H. Bentley, *The Humanists and Holy Writ: New Testament Scholarship in the Renaissance* (Princeton, 1983); A. J. Brown, 'The Date of Erasmus' Latin Translation of the New Testament', *Transactions of the Cambridge Bibliographical Society* 8 (1984) 351–380; G. Dogaer, *Flemish Miniature Painting in the 15th and 16th Centuries* (Amsterdam, 1987); A. Reeve, *Erasmus' Annotations on the New Testament: The Gospels* (London, 1986); W. Schwarz, *Principles and Problems of Biblical Translation* (Cambridge, 1955), chap. 5; J. B. Trapp, 'Notes on Manuscripts Written by Peter Meghen', *The Book Collector,* 24 (1975) 80–96; 'John Colet, His Manuscripts and the Ps.-Dionysius' in *Classical Influences on European Culture, A.D. 1500–1700,* ed. R. R. Bolgar (Cambridge, 1976), pp. 205–221, at 208–210; 'John Colet' in *Contemporaries of Erasmus: A Biographical Register of the Renaissance and Reformation,* 3 vols., ed. P. Bietenholtz (Toronto, 1985) 1.324–28.

[1]Reeve, p. 241, 1535 edition. The 'codex aureus' is El Escorial, Real Biblioteca de San Lorenzo, MS Vitr. 17, an eleventh-century gospelbook: see G. Antolín, *Catalogo de los codices latinos de la real Biblioteca del Escorial,* 5 vols. (Madrid, 1910–23) 4.280–82.

Amen amen dico vobis, non Moses dedit vobis illũ panem de celo, sed pater meus dat vobis panẽ de celo verum. Panis enim dei est qui de celo descendit, et dat vitam mundo. Dixerunt ergo ad eum: Domine, semper da nobis panem istum. Dixit autem eis IESVS. Ego sũ panis ille vite. Qui venit ad me, non esuriet: et qui credit in me, non sitiet vnquam.

Amen amen dico vobis: non moyses dedit vobis panem de celo: sed pater meus dat vobis panem de celo verum. Panis enim verus est qui de celo descendit et dat vitã mundo. Dixerunt ergo ad eum. Domine: semp da nobis panẽ hunc. Dixit autem eis IESVS. Ego sum panis vite. Qui venit ad me non esuriet: et q̃ credit in me non sitiet in eter

27. The Complutensian Polyglot (Arnaldus Guillelmus de Brocario, Alcalá 1514–17, 1520): Princeton, N.J., William H. Scheide Library, Princeton University Library, Scheide Collection 8.2.9.

Cardinal Ximénez's six-volume Bible is a typographical *tour-de-force:* not unreasonably was the printer described as 'artis *impressorie* magist(er)'.[1] It presents the Latin Vulgate in parallel with the Septuagint and the original Hebrew (vols. 3–6). For the Pentateuch only (vol. 3), the Aramaic exegetical paraphrase or 'targum' is given at the foot of the page, with its own Latin translation. The New Testament volume (1) has the Vulgate in parallel with the Greek; and the second volume provides grammatical and lexical assistance with Hebrew and a substantial Greek-Latin glossary. The epithet 'Complutensian' derives from the Roman town of Complutum, the site of Ximénez's new university of Alcalá de Henares, where the work was undertaken.

Paper; page 357 x 259 mm.; text 293 x 220 mm.; central column 212 x 37 mm.; 54 lines of Latin; 27 lines of Hebrew. No colored rubrication, decorated initials or formal illumination.

In the page shown (Exod. 31:14–32:4) the 'translatio beati Hieronymi', the traditional Vulgate Bible, is the central column—hanging (in the words of Ximénez's Prologue to the Reader) like Christ between the two thieves: on its right the Septuagint with a Latin interlinear translation, on its left the Hebrew. The reader whose Hebrew is less than fluent may follow the sequence of Latin letters above the Hebrew lines; these are repeated at the appropriate point in the Latin text. In the first line, for example, superscript **q** and **r** lead to 'morte' (**q**), 'moriatur' (**r**). The more practiced reader, who wishes to consult a Hebrew dictionary, will find the roots ('primitiua') of compound words hung in the outer margin of the line in which they occur. The same assistance is provided for the 'translatio chaldaica' (sc. Aramaic) at the foot of the page. This philological zeal and indeed sophistication in the Hebrew contrasts with the fundamental conservatism of the whole enterprise: the privileged text is Jerome's Vulgate, as good a Vulgate text as could be established, but not a direct version of the Hebrew, nor, for the New Testament, a direct version of the Greek.

The work was completed in the three years 1514–17, beginning with the New Testament (10 January, 1514). The delay of several years before its publication was primarily due to the death of Ximenes (1517), rather than—as might appear—the imperial privilege protecting the *Nouum instrumentum* (**no. 26**).[2]

Bibliography: J. H. Bentley, *The Humanists and Holy Writ: New Testament Scholarship in the Renaissance* (Princeton, 1983), pp. 70–111; B. Botfield, *Praefationes et epistolae editionibus principibus auctorum ueterum praepositae* (Cambridge, 1861) [prologues to Leo X and to the Reader]; J. P. R. Lyell, *Cardinal Ximenes* (London, 1917), chap. IV; F. J. Norton, *A Descriptive Catalogue of Printing in Spain and Portugal, 1501-1520* (Cambridge, 1978), no. 27.

[1] Colophon to lib. VI.

[2] Erasmus's privilege is published on the title page of the *editio princeps* of the *Nouum instrumentum* (1516): 'Cum priuilegio Maximiliani Caesaris Augusti. ne quis alius in sacra romani imperii ditione intra quatuor annos excudat. aut alibi exclusum importet'. See also Erasmus's letter to Willibald Pirckheimer (*Opus epistolarum des. Erasmi Roterdami,* ed. P. S. Allen, 12 vols. [Oxford, 1906–1958], ep. 1341, 5.202). For Arnao Guillén de Brocar, the printer, see Norton, pp. 159–61. For the irregular and uncertain operation of book-privilege in the early sixteenth century, see E. Armstrong, *Before Copyright: The French Book-Privilege System 1498–1526* (Cambridge, 1990), pp. 13–15.

Trāsla. Gre. lxx. cū interp. latina.

vobis. q polluerit illud: morte morietur. ois
ὑμῖν. ὁ βεβηλῶν αὐτό, θανάτῳ θανατωθήσεται. πᾶς
qui faciet in eo opus: peribit ani
ὅστις ποιήσει ἐν αὐτῷ ἔργον, ἐξολοθρευθήσεται ἡ ψυ-
ma illa de medio ppli sui. sex di-
χὴ ἐκείνη ἐκ μέσου τοῦ λαοῦ αὐτῆς. ἓξ ἡμέ-
es facies opa: at die septima
ρας ποιήσεις ἔργα, τῇ δὲ ἡμέρᾳ τῇ ἑβδόμῃ
sabbata requies sancta dño. ois
σάββατα ἀνάπαυσις ἁγία τῷ κυρίῳ. πᾶς
qui faciet op9 die sabbatoꝝ:
ὅστις ποιήσει ἔργον τῇ ἡμέρᾳ τῶν σαββάτων,
morietur. et custodient filij israel
θανατωθήσεται. καὶ φυλάξουσιν οἱ υἱοὶ ἰσραὴλ
sabbata facere ipsa in gñatiões su-
τὰ σάββατα ποιεῖν αὐτὰ εἰς τὰς γενεὰς αὐ-
as. testamētū eternū in me et filijs isra
τῶν. διαθήκη αἰώνιος ἐν ἐμοὶ καὶ τοῖς υἱοῖς ἰσ-
el: signū est sēpiternū. qm̄ in sex dieb9
ραὴλ, σημεῖόν ἐστιν αἰώνιον. ὅτι ἐν ἓξ ἡμέραις
fecit dñs et celū et terrā: et
ἐποίησε κύριος τόν τε οὐρανὸν καὶ τὴν γῆν, καὶ
die septima cessauit et requieuit.
τῇ ἡμέρᾳ τῇ ἑβδόμῃ ἐπαύσατο καὶ κατέπαυ-
et dedit moysi qñ cessauit loqui
σε. καὶ ἔδωκε μωυσῇ ἡνίκα κατέπαυσε λαλῶν
ei in mōte sina duas tabulas
αὐτῷ ἐν τῷ ὄρει τῷ σινᾷ τὰς δύο πλάκας
testamēti: tabulas lapideas scriptas
τοῦ μαρτυρίου, πλάκας λιθίνας γεγραμμένας
digito dei.
τῷ δακτύλῳ τοῦ θεοῦ.

Ca. 32.

Et vidēs popul9: q tardauit moyses
καὶ ἰδὼν ὁ λαός, ὅτι κεχρόνικε μωυσῆς
descendere de mōte: cōgregat9 ē ppl's ad aa-
καταβῆναι ἐκ τοῦ ὄρους, συνέστη ὁ λαὸς ἐπὶ ἀα-
ron: et dicunt ei: surge: et fac no
ρών, καὶ λέγουσιν αὐτῷ, ἀνάστηθι, καὶ ποίησον ἡ-
bis deos: q precedant nos. nā moy-
μῖν θεούς, οἳ προπορεύσονται ἡμῶν. ὁ γὰρ μωυ-
ses hic homo q eduxit nos de terra
σῆς οὗτος ὁ ἄνθρωπος ὃς ἐξήγαγεν ἡμᾶς ἐκ γῆς
egypti: nō scim9 qd factū ē illi. et di-
αἰγύπτου, οὐκ οἴδαμεν τί γέγονεν αὐτῷ. καὶ λέ-
cit illis aaron: tollite inaures aureas
γει αὐτοῖς ἀαρών, περιέλεσθε τὰ ἐνώτια τὰ χρυσᾶ
q in aurib9 mulierū vraꝝ et filiaꝝ: et
τὰ ἐν τοῖς ὠσὶ τῶν γυναικῶν ὑμῶν καὶ θυγατέρων, καὶ
afferte ad me. et abstulerūt ois popul9 in-
ἐνέγκατε πρός με. καὶ περιείλαντο πᾶς ὁ λαὸς τὰ ἐνώ-
aures aureas q in aurib9 eorū: et attulerūt
τια τὰ χρυσᾶ τὰ ἐν τοῖς ὠσὶν αὐτῶν, καὶ ἤνεγκαν
ad aaron. et accepit de manib9 illoꝝ
πρὸς ἀαρών. καὶ ἐδέξατο ἐκ τῶν χειρῶν αὐτῶν

Trāsla. B. Hiero.

vobis. Qui polluerit il
lud: morte moriatur.
Qui fecerit in eo op9:
peribit anima
illius de medio populi
sui. Sex diebus
facietis opus: in die se
ptimo
sabbatum est requies
sancta dño. Omnis
qui fecerit opus ī hac
die:
morietur. Custodiant
filii israel
sabbatum: & celebrēt
illud
in gñatiōibus suis. Pa-
ctū est sempiternū inter
me & filios israel: si-
gnūq; perpetuum. sex
enim diebus fecit do-
minus
celum & terram: & in
septimo ab omni ope-
re cessauit. Deditq; do
minus moysi
cōpletis huiuscemodi
sermonibus in mōte si
nai duas tabulas testi-
mōii lapideas: scriptas
digito dei. Ca. 32.
Uides āt ppl's q
moram faceret moyses
descendēdi de monte:
congregatus aduersus
aaron dixit.
Surge fac nobis deos
qui
nos precedant. Moysi
enim huic viro
qui nos eduxit de ter-
ra egypti: ignoramus
quid acciderit. Dixit-
q; ad eos
aaron. Tollite inaures
aureas de
vxorū filiorūq; & filia-
rū vestrarū auribus: &
afferte ad me. Fecit po-
pulus q iusserat deferēs
inaures
ad aarō. Quas cū ille
accepisset: formauit

Tex. Heb. Exo. Ca. xxxij. Primitiua. heb.

לכם מחלליה מות יומת כי כל
העשה בה מלאכה ונכרתה הנפש
ההוא מקרב עמיה: ששת ימים
יעשה מלאכה וביום השביעי
שבת שבתון קדש ליהוה כל
העשה מלאכה ביום השבת מות
יומת: ושמרו בני ישראל את
השבת לעשות את השבת
לדרתם ברית עולם: ביני ובין
בני ישראל אות הוא לעלם כי
ששת ימים עשה יהוה את
השמים ואת הארץ וביום השביעי
שבת וינפש: ויתן אל משה
ככלתו לדבר אתו בהר סיני שני
לחת העדת לחת אבן כתבים
באצבע אלהים: וירא העם כי
בשש משה לרדת מן ההר
ויקהל העם על אהרן ויאמרו
אליו קום עשה לנו אלהים אשר
ילכו לפנינו כי זה משה האיש
אשר העלנו מארץ מצרים לא
ידענו מה היה לו: ויאמר אלהם
אהרן פרקו נזמי הזהב אשר באזני
נשיכם בניכם ובנתיכם והביאו
אלי: ויתפרקו כל העם את נזמי
הזהב אשר באזניהם ויביאו
אל אהרן: ויקח מידם ויצר

חלל
לאו כרת
יום
שבע
דור ברת עלם
בנה
יום
נפש נתן
כלה שנה
לוח עוד
צבע

Cap. xxxii.

ראה ירד
קהל אמר
פנה
עלה
נשה בוא
פרק
לקח

Transla. Chal.

לכון דיחליניה אתקטלא יתקטיל ארי כל דיעביד בה עבידתא וישתיציא אנשא ה…
מגו עמיה: שתא יומין תתעביד עבידתא וביומא שביעאה שבת שבתא קודשא ק…
ייי כל דיעביד עבידתא ביומא דשבתא אתקטלא יתקטיל: ויטרון בני ישראל …
שבתא למעבד ית שבתא לדריהון קיים עלם: בין מימרי ובין בני ישראל את …
לעלם ארי בשתא יומין עבד ייי ית שמיא וית ארעא וביומא שביעאה שבת ונ…
ויהב למשה כד שיצי למללא עמיה בטורא דסיני תרין לוחי סהדותא לוחי א…
כתיבין באצבעא דייי: Ca. xxxii. וחזא עמא ארי אוחר משה למי…
מן טורא ואתכניש עמא על אהרן ואמרו ליה קום עבד לנא דחלן דיהכון קדמנא א…
דין משה גברא דאסקנא מארעא דמצרים לא ידענא מה הוה ליה: ואמר להון א…
פריקו קדשי דדהבא די באודני נשיכון בניכון ובנתיכון ואיתיאו לותי: ואתפריקו …
כל עמא ית קדשי דדהבא די באודניהון ואיתיו לות אהרן: ונסיב מידיהון וצר …

Interp. chal.

vobis: qui prophanauerit illud morte moriatur: qm̄ oīs qui fecerit in eo opus exterminabitur homo ille de medio populi sui. Sex diebus fiet opus: in die autem septimo sabbatū est reqes sancta corā dño. Quicūq; fecerit opus in die sabbati: morte moriatur. Custodiantq; filij israel sabbatū: vt celebrent sabbatū in gñationibus suis. Pactū eternū est īter verbū meū et inter filios israel: signū est in eternū: qm̄ in sex diebus fecit dñs celum ⁊ terrā: ⁊ in die septimo quieuit et requieuit. Deditq; moysi cum cōsumasset loqui cū eo in monte sinai duas tabulas testimonij tabulas lapideas scriptas digito dei. Ca. 32.

Uiditq; populus q moram faceret moyses vt descenderet de monte: ⁊ congregatus est ppl's ad aarō: ⁊ dixerūt ei. Surge fac nobis deos q gradiant ante nos. Moysi eniz huic viro q eduxit nos de terra egypti nescim9 qd acciderit. Dixitq; eis aaron. Tollite inaures aureas q sunt in auribus vxoꝝ vestrarū: filioꝝ ⁊ filiarū vraꝝ ⁊ afferte ad me. Tuleruntq; oīs popul9 inaures aureas q erant in auribus suis: ⁊ detulerūt ad aaron. et tulit de manib9 eoꝝ: ⁊ formauit

Primitiua chal.

חלל קטל
שצא שית
נטר
עבד קום אמר
נוח
צבע אחר נחת
כנש
נסק
נשה בנה אתא
פרק צור

28. Luther's Translation of the New Testament from the Greek Original, Published by Melchior Lotther in Wittenberg, September 1522: London, British Library, C.36.g.7, fol. lxix^{v}.

Luther's enforced retreat in the Wartburg (1520) gave him the opportunity to translate Erasmus's Greek text of 1516—the *Novum instrumentum* (**no. 26**).

Paper; v + 77 + xxix fol.; page 301 x 193 mm.; 44 lines. Fine contemporary stamped leather binding. The text of the Apocalypse (fol. vi–xxxiv) includes twenty-one full-page woodcuts by Lucas Cranach the Elder, or his workshop (Volz, pp. 111–19). These are fully integrated in the text, which continues on the verso of each picture.

Luther's 'Septembertestament', to be followed by sections of the Old Testament throughout the 1520s and the *editio princeps* of the whole Bible in 1534, replaced the German rendering of the Vulgate, which had a continuous history from the ninth century onwards (see **nos. 9** and **12**). The *editio princeps* by Johannes Mentelin of Strassburg in 1466 (Kurrelmeyer) is a splendid folio volume that was widely influential over the next half-century.[1] But Mentelin's text stays close to the Latin syntax, in the manner of the Wycliffite Bible (**no. 23**), whereas Luther used the spoken German of his own day. The degree of divergence may be seen in Mentelin's text of John 6:32–34, with those words italicized in which Luther (lines 23–27 opposite) diverges from Mentelin's Vulgate:

> *Dorumb* sprach Ihesus zu yhn / *Gewerlich gewerlich /* sag ichs euch / Moyses *gab* euch nit *das* brot vom himel / *wann* mein vatter gibt euch das *gewer* brot vom himel / *wann das gewer* brot gotz *ist* / das *do nidersteigt* vom himel / und gibt das leben der werlte.
> *Dorumb* sy sprachen zum im / *O* herr / gib uns *zeallen zeyten ditz* brot.[2]

Luther's translation was at once more accurate and more accessible than the German Vulgate. It was also consciously polemical, both in the Apocalypse illustrations—in which the Beast from the sea wears a papal tiara (Volz)—and more insidiously in his rendering of the key texts relating to justification by faith.

Bibliography: W. Kurrelmeyer, *Die erste deutsche Bibel,* 2 vols. (Bibliothek des Litterarischen Vereins in Stuttgart, 234, 266, Tübingen, 1904–1915) [= Mentelin Bible]; Luther, *Sendbrief vom Dolmetschen* [an 'open letter about translation']; F. Tschirch, *1200 Jahre deutsche Sprache* (Berlin, 1955) [parallel text samples of Evangelienwerk, Mentelin and Luther]; H. Volz and H. Blanke, *D. Martin Luther: Die gantze Heilige Schrifft. Deutsch, Wittenberg 1545,* 2 vols. (Munich, 1972) [= Luther Bible in its final state]. H. Bluhm, 'Bedeutung und Eigenart von Luthers Septembertestament: Zum 450 Jubiläum' in *Studies in Luther: Luther Studien* (Bern, 1987), pp. 53–75; H. Reinitzer, *Deutsche Bibelübersetzungen des Mittelalters* (Vestigia Bibliae, 9–10; Bern, 1991) [Note Kornrumpf and Gärtner on the 'Klosterneuburger Evangelienwerk']; W. Schwarz, as **no. 26** above; H. Volz, *Martin Luthers deutsche Bibel* (Hamburg, 1978); C. J. Wells, *German: A Linguistic History to 1945* (Oxford, 1985, pp. 190–98.

[1] A fine two-column folio, with the whole Bible in a single volume (BMC 1.52; GWD 4295; Goff B-624).

[2] Therefore Jesus spoke to them 'Verily, verily, I say to you Moses did not give you the bread of heaven, for my father gives you the true bread of heaven. For the true bread is God's, which descends from heaven and gives life to the world.' Then they said to him, 'O Lord, give us this bread at all times'.

am lande / da sie hyn furen.

Des andern tags / sahe das volck das ihensid des meers stund / das keyn ander schiff daselbs war / denn das eynige* daryn seyne iunger getretten waren / vnnd das Jhesus nicht mit seynen iungern ynn das schiff tretten war / sondern alleyn seyne iunger waren weg gefaren / Es kamen aber ander schiff vō Tiberias nahe zu der stett / da sie das brod gessen hatten vnnd dem hern gedanckt / Da nu das volck sahe / das Jhesus nicht da war / noch seyne iunger / tratten sie auch ynn die schiff / vnd kamen gen Capernaum / vnd suchten Jhesū.

Vnnd da sie yhn funden ihensid des meers / sprachen sie zu yhm / Meyster / wenne bistu her komen? Jhesus antwort yhn vnd sprach / warlich warlich / ich sage euch / yhr sucht mich nitt darumb das yhr zeychen gesehen habt / sondern / das yhr von dem brod gessen habt vñ seytt satt worden / wircket speysz / nicht die da verdirbt / sondern die da bleybt ynn das ewige leben / wilche euch des menschen son geben wirt / denn den selbigen hatt Gott der vater versigelt.

(versigellt) Das ist / mit dem heyligen geyst begabt / das wer die speys isset (wie folget) auch den geyst entfehet vnd leben soll.

Da sprachen sie zu yhm / was sollen wyr thun / das wyr Gottis werck wircken? Jhesus antwort vñ sprach zu yhn / das ist Gottis werck / dz yhr an den glewbet / den er gesand hat / da sprachen sie zu yhm / was thustu denn fur eyn zeychen / auff das wyr sehen vnd glewben dyr? was wirckistu? vnser vetter haben hymel brod gessen ynn der wusten / wie geschriebē stehet / Er gab yhn brod vom hymel zu essen / Psa
Da sprach Jhesus zu yhn / warlich warlich / ich sage euch / Moses hat euch nicht brod vom hymel geben / sondern meyn vatter gibt euch das rechte brod vom hymel / denn dis ist das brod Gotis / das vom hymel kompt / vnd gibt der wellt das leben.

Da sprachen sie zu yhm / Herre / gib vns allwege solch brod / Jhesus aber sprach zu yhn / ich bynn das brod des lebens / wer zu myr kompt / den wirt nicht hungern / vnd wer an mich glewbet / den wirtt nymer mehr dursten / Aber ich habs euch gesagt / das yhr mich gesehen habt vnd glewbet doch nicht / Alles was myr meyn vater gibt / das kompt zu myr / vnnd wer zu myr kompt / den werd ich nicht hynaus stossen / denn ich bynn vom hymel komen / nicht das ich meynen willē thu / sondern des / der mich gesand hat / Das ist aber der wille des vatters der mich gesand hatt / das ich nichts verliere von allem das er myr geben hatt / szondern das ichs aufferwecke am iungsten tag / Das ist aber der wille des / der mich gesand hatt / das / wer den son sihet vnd glewbet an yhn / habe das ewige leben / vnnd ich werd yhn aufferwecken am iungsten tage.

Da murretē die Juden / daruber / das er sagete / Ich byn das brod das vom hymel komen ist / vnnd sprachen / ist diser nicht Jhesus Josephs son / des vater vnd mutter wyr kennen? wie spricht er denn / ich bynn vom hymel komen? Jhesus antwort vnd sprach zu yhn / murret nicht vnternander / Es kan niemandt zu myr komen / es sey denn /

das yhn

GLOSSARY

AD COLLATIONEM: Text to be read aloud at monastic meal-times, *lit.* 'at dinner'.

ADOPTIONISM: Definition that Jesus, as a human being, was the 'adopted' rather than the natural son of God the Father. By contrast Christ the 'Logos', or word of God, was eternal and equal with God the Father; in art, Father and 'Logos' might be shown as two identical figures, e.g. creating the world. This theological position, which was current in Spain in the late eighth century, was condemned at the court of Charlemagne.

CANTICLES: Six passages from the Old Testament (e.g. the Canticle of Habbakuk: Habbakuk 3), one intertestamental (the *Benedicite*) and three from the New Testament (*Benedictus, Magnificat* and *Nunc dimittis:* Luke 1–2) which, as recurring elements in the monastic liturgy, often formed an appendix to the Psalter. 'The Canticle' can also designate The Song of Songs (unwisely, in my view).

CAPITULA: A list of chapters (*sing.* 'capitulum') preceding a text, to show its internal divisions.

CAROLINGIAN MINUSCULE: A clear, legible script that was developed in the late eighth century, at first in a few centers and then gradually adopted throughout the Empire of Charlemagne and his successors as the standard text hand. A late version of the hand provided the first model for the 'humanistic' script that developed in Florence in the late fourteenth and early fifteenth centuries.

COLOPHON: A note at the end of a manuscript or printed book—generally no more than one or two sentences—indicating the date, place and/or circumstances in which that volume was written.

DOMINICAL WORDS: That part of the Gospel text which is attributed directly to Jesus, e.g. the Beatitudes (Matthew 5) and the Words from the Cross (Matthew 27, etc.).

DUCTUS: The total impression left by a page of script, having regard to the angle of the strokes and the order in which they were made. See the fine definition by James J. John, 'Latin Palaeography' in *Medieval Studies: An Introduction,* ed. J. M. Powell (Syracuse, 1976), p. 6.

EDITIO PRINCEPS: The first ('princeps') printed edition of a text.

ELEGIACS: A Latin verse-form consisting of a six-foot line (hexameter), followed by a five-foot line (pentameter), and so alternating indefinitely. A classic practitioner is Ovid.

FLOURISHING: Penwork decoration giving greater prominence to an initial, e.g. at the beginning of a new chapter of text. The practice is widespread from the mid-twelfth century onwards, the colors being normally red alternating with blue.

FLYLEAVES: Leaves added at the beginning or the end of a manuscript in the process of binding or rebinding. They may be scrap parchment or paper preserving a random fragment of an older text, or a blank sheet on which later owners or readers have left miscellaneous notes. The outside leaf that is glued onto the binding is termed a pastedown.

HEXAPLA: The text of the Old Testament with six versions in parallel that was established by Origen in the mid-third century. The versions are the Hebrew text in Hebrew characters, the Hebrew text transliterated into Greek characters, and four Greek versions, including the Septuagint. Jerome knew the Hexapla, but by the time of Cassiodorus it had vanished.

INSULAR: A term applied to script and illumination produced in the British Isles (including Ireland) from the seventh to ninth centuries. By extension it may be applied to the work of scribes and illuminators in Irish and Anglo-Saxon foundations in Continental Europe over the same period.

LEMMATA: Brief quotations from the text, set at the beginning of a gloss or within a commentary to identify the passage to which the gloss or commentary relates. A *lemma* is often underlined in red.

NECROLOGY: A list of deceased members of a monastic community, or others for whom the community has agreed to pray. The names will be listed by date of death, January-December, with no indication of the year of death.

PANDECT: A single volume containing a complete collection of related books (i.e. a *corpus*). The earliest use relates to the Bible (see Cassiodorus); from the twelfth century onwards the term also applies to Civil and Canon Law.

PASTEDOWN. See FLYLEAVES.

PATRISTIC: Relating to the Greek and Latin writings of the Early Church: e.g. Ambrose, Jerome and Augustine (late fourth–early fifth centuries) and finally Gregory the Great (*ob.* 604).

QUIRE: A physical section of a manuscript or printed book, made either by folding a large sheet of parchment/paper once (= a bifolium, a quire of two), twice and cutting it (= a quaternion, a quire of four) and so on upwards, or by placing ready-cut bifolia one on top of the other and then folding. An early medieval quire is commonly of eight, and a later medieval quire of ten, twelve and above.

ROMANUM TEXT OF THE PSALTER: Jerome's earliest revision of the Psalter, in which he made some use of the Greek Septuagint but none of the Hebrew original. It remained in liturgical use until the late eighth century in Northern Europe, and until much later elsewhere. In England it was superseded only at the Norman Conquest.

RUSTIC CAPITALS: A form used in *de luxe* manuscripts and painted inscriptions (e.g. at Pompeii) in Late Antiquity, it was later adopted as display writing in manuscripts. It was widely used by Carolingian scribes, and in a somewhat aetiolated form into the eleventh-century and later.

SINGLETON: A single leaf in the body of a manuscript which is not physically joined to another leaf in a quire.

SYNOPTICS: The Gospels of Matthew, Mark and Luke, as opposed to John.

TAWED LEATHER: Animal skin (normally sheep and calf) stripped of the bristles and cured with alum and salt, giving a suede-like white surface. It is commonly used in western book-bindings from the eleventh century to the mid-fifteenth.

TEXTUALIS: Any relatively formal script used from the twelfth century to the fifteenth which is appropriate to a library text rather than to a legal or other document. The term is also used as a synonym for Gothic bookhand.

TIRONIAN NOTES: A system of shorthand named from Cicero's secretary, Tiro. It was used in the Roman lawcourts, by notaries and in Late Antiquity by episcopal clerks. Carolingian scholars rediscovered and adapted the system for the annotation of school texts and as reference-signs linking text to gloss.

TRIDENTINE: Relating to the Council of Trent, the nine sessions of which (1545–63) provided a point of reference for Roman Catholic legislation and practice for the next three centuries.

UNCIAL: A formal Late Roman text hand—rounded by contrast with rustic capitals—which was mainly, though not exclusively, used for Christian texts. It had a particular influence on Anglo-Saxon script of the seventh and eighth centuries (see **no. 3**).

INDEX

MANUSCRIPTS BY NAME

MANUSCRIPTS BY LOCATION

PRINTED BOOKS in specific copies

ABOUT THE AUTHOR

Margaret T. Gibson received her Ph.D. from Oxford University. She is currently Senior Research Fellow at St. Peter's College, Oxford University. In addition to *The Bible in the Latin West* she has published nine other books and numerous articles. Her most recent works are *Joseph Mayer of Liverpool, The Schools and the Cloister: The Life and Work of Alexander Nequam,* and *English Romanesque Art 1066–1200: Exhibition Guide.* Gibson is also a Fellow of the Medieval Academy of America.